N⁰ 1

More Than One Life

A Nottinghamshire Childhood
with D.H.Lawrence

ENID HOPKIN HILTON

ALAN SUTTON

First published in the United Kingdom in 1993 by
Alan Sutton Publishing Limited
Phoenix Mill · Far Thrupp · Stroud · Gloucestershire

First published in the United States of America in 1993 by
Alan Sutton Publishing Inc · 83 Washington Street · Dover · NH 03820

British Library Cataloguing in Publication Data

Hilton, Enid
More Than One Life: Nottinghamshire
Childhood with D.H. Lawrence
I. Title
942.5208092

ISBN 0 7509-0314-7

Library of Congress Cataloging in Publication Data

Hilton, Enid Hopkin, 1895-
More than one life: a Nottinghamshire childhood with D.H. Lawrence/Enid Hopkin
Hilton.
p. cm.
Includes bibliographical references.
ISBN 0–7509–0314–7:$26.00
1. Lawrence, D.H. (David Herbert), 1885-1930—Friends and associates. 2. Lawrence,
D.H. (David Herbert), 1885-1930—Biography—Youth. 3. Nottinghamshire
(England)—Social life and customs. 4. Hilton, Enid Hopkin, 1895- —Childhood and
youth. 5. Authors, English—20th century—Biography. 6. Nottinghamshire
(England)—Biography. I. Title.
PR6023.A93Z6314 1993
823'.912—dc20
[B] 92-46030
CIP

Typeset in 12/14 Garamond
Typesetting and origination by
Alan Sutton Publishing Limited.
Printed in Great Britain by
The Bath Press, Avon.

Contents

Cobwebs in the Sky

Foreword

Enid Hilton remembered first meeting D.H. Lawrence when she was five and he just over fifteen years old, 'a lanky, rather sickly-looking young man' with 'most peculiar, disturbing' eyes. After he grew a moustache, she wrote to me, he reminded her of the mad hatter in *Alice in Wonderland*.

Over the first few years she appears on and off in his correspondence, named at first in his letters to her parents Willie and Sallie Hopkin, such occasional references making way later for frequent mentions of her name. A substantial number of letters are addressed to her at the time when she played a vital part in the clandestine storage and distribution in England of copies of *Lady Chatterley's Lover*. She had previously, after a visit to Lawrence at Sandicci near Florence, carried to England some of his pictures exhibited in 1929 at the Warren Gallery and seized by the police.

She contributed to Edward Nehls' *Composite Biography* valuable information on the social and intellectual background of her family circle at the time of Lawrence's adolescence. Her mother, Sallie Potter, the sister of a close Sheffield friend of Edward Carpenter, was 'rarely mistaken in her impression of people', Enid wrote to me, adding: 'Lawrence brought all of his women immediately to my mother for her reaction to them.' Willie Hopkin was a keen seeker for new horizons in society and ethics. In their Eastwood home, described with a touch of irony in *Mr Noon* as the house of Lewis and Patty Goddard, they entertained socialists, for example Ramsay MacDonald and Margaret Bondfield, theosophists such as Charlotte Despard, reformers of sex and society like Edward Carpenter and Sylvia Pankhurst. During the First World War, alderman Willie Hopkin was chairman of a local tribunal before which conscientious objectors had to appear.

Sallie Hopkin was an active feminist like her intimate friend Alice Dax. After she died Enid took over from her the role of Mrs Dax's confidant. On Alice's love affair with Lawrence she is the only source of reliable evidence. If only for that her memoirs would contribute decisively to our knowledge of a period of the writer's life on which the discretion of his sister long maintained a cloud of mystery. Her memories of her childhood and adolescence will enable readers better to understand the social and ethical environment of young Lawrence in late Victorian and Edwardian days.

Emile Delavenay
Honorary Professor
University of Nice

Dedication

This book is dedicated to the fond memory of my father and mother, William and Sallie Hopkin. Sallie left us many years ago in the early 1920s. William lived to the ripe age of ninety, when he collapsed while lecturing to a group of young people. Mother left through illness, father with his boots on.

In my childhood days, as at the present time, I think of them as two wonderful people always ready to adventure, physically, mentally, and spiritually. As D.H. Lawrence commented in his letter after Sallie's death, they led a rather remarkable life of adventure that was not limited by their personal differences in temperament and interests. William always wanted to see around the next corner or beyond the next mountain. He was never disappointed when such a corner revealed yet another corner or the conquering of one mountain exposed yet more mountains ahead.

Out walking, Sallie, the practical one, pursed her lips tightly together and informed William and me it was time to go home to afternoon tea. William always remarked he simply had to see what was around the next turn in the road or what the disclosed valley was like when one reached the top of some mountain. At quite an early age I remembered noting that in the end we turned the corner or climbed the hill, Mother's practicality giving way to her own imagination stimulated by my father. In this way a sense of adventure was rarely lost. Thus, through conflict and agreement and their mutual understanding, I received a magical childhood filled with the early morning joys of hunting fairy rings and the beauty of the heather-covered Yorkshire moors that we always walked over in August. When we reached the ocean we spent our days walking the coast to the next fishing village, exploring rock pools or finding strange seaweeds that we took with us until they rotted and the smell was so terrific that Mother insisted they be discarded, but by that time it did not matter. We had had the joy of finding the seaweed and dragging it along with us.

If I became tired on our long walks my father would tell strange fairy tales about the flowers and the birds and the country through which we were passing, and my legs no longer ached. Hunting for violets, honeysuckle in hedgerows at home, exploring rock pools at the seashore, for these I am eternally grateful.

Not only did my parents stimulate a keen appreciation of physical beauty and an eager sense of adventure, but they aroused in me a lifelong love of poetry. My father, himself quite a good poet, always carried in his pocket the *Oxford Book of English Verse*. If we stopped to rest a few minutes on our walks out came the book and my father, in his gentle voice, read the poems. Or if Mother was busy sewing and I was occupied with my homework, again the book would appear and I listened to the narrative poems of the old masters. Many of these I knew by heart and many I still know.

The scent of heather on a warm day over the Yorkshire moors, the magnificent, almost overwhelming, sunsets over the ocean, the miles of flower-covered pastures with cows and horses gently grazing, the beauty and adventure of poetry . . . who could ask more of his or her parents? Few ask as much, not understanding.

Introduction

There was an old woman tossed up in a basket,
Ninety times as high as the moon,
And where she was going I couldn't but ask it,
For in her hand she carried a broom.
'Old woman, old woman, old woman,' quoth I,
'Whither, oh whither, and why so high?'
'To sweep the cobwebs off the sky.'
'May I go with thee?'
'Aye, by and by.'

My memory of the nursery rhyme may not be absolutely correct, but, as with most such verses, this one covers a profound truth. And in the case of D.H. Lawrence the cobwebs mentioned always appeared to me to have caught the author in an inextricable web created by some of his biographers, leaving only the skeleton. Most of these biographers missed the essential person, their writings seeming not to be concerned with the real Lawrence. They suggest a personality which I never encountered.

I first met Lawrence in our town of Eastwood, Nottinghamshire.

I was a five-year-old child, an age when most children begin to be conscious of things and people beyond themselves. I remained in touch with this man, sometimes closely, until shortly before his death in 1930. Through these long years the individual I knew was gentle, kind, and full of insights; he always had time, energy, and understanding for a little girl growing up in a difficult and changing world. He could, and often did, take time to help a student, never very good at mathematics, solve the problems in her homework and throw light on the dark places in arithmetic and later in algebra. He was also the person who opened doors of observation by his own miraculous feeling about a rock or even a pebble, a flower or the curve in a blade of grass. For me, the secret of association with Lawrence was a strange power that caused him to raise even the commonplace everyday things of life into a new sphere of beauty, importance, and order. This is a quality that made him special in the lives of so many and earned him a place with the 'greats' of Westminster Abbey.

At the same time this extraordinary quality in the man led to misunderstandings in the early days of his first books. Lawrence's books convey that heightened view of people, things, and life itself, especially during the period when England was recovering from the stodgy onslaughts of Victorianism, which tended to condemn new ideas, undeveloped philosophies, and indeed any previously unacknowledged versions of truth. The time in which Lawrence's books appeared was one of change from these stuffy attitudes to a broader view of life. My quarrel with most books on Lawrence, many of which have emerged since his death, is that they take their views almost solely from other books or later gossip, without their authors having known or even met their subject himself. They tell us little of the complex simplicity that made him both a delightful companion, at his best full of fun, and almost always one who opened doors to future thought and understanding.

My conception of Lawrence is very different from the average one because it is largely the view of the child and the young woman. To me he was extraordinarily kind and patient, and very helpful. He tried his best to lift me out of the stilted English atmosphere of my upbringing and into the broader world of life and of literature. And he did, for through him I met Katherine Mansfield, Middleton Murry, Aldous Huxley, Koteliansky, the Brewsters, and others. I was awfully fond of Lawrence. He was rather on a par with my father, to whom I was very close. Lawrence never tore me down, as clever adults are prone to do with children. I feel it is very important that this vision be shown to the world.

In my account of D.H. Lawrence there is considerable justification for almost an excessive use of autobiography. He had already experienced the world I lived in and the foolish social and other restrictions. The years between us were few, but Lawrence knew that my life also required a new look of freedom. I doubt if he seriously contemplated that his attempts to free people would eventually lead to the sort of licence that has become part of the human system. If he did he might have felt it was part of human development, a 'phase' to be gone through, to be adjusted later. I do feel, however, that if he had lived into the present world and time he would be horrified at our descent from freedom into moral breakdown and chaos.

One day I was standing by the big window in the living room of our house in Eastwood. There were many people in the room, including Lawrence. He walked up behind me: 'Enid, what are you looking at?' I told him that I was just looking, at nothing in particular. He pointed through the window: 'Out there is a great big, exciting world. Why don't you go and see it?' So I did. It has not been an easy exploration and is rarely comfortable. Lawrence was never interested in ease or comfort, but in the exploration itself.

Before these explorations began, Lawrence and I were raised in the same town of Eastwood, Nottinghamshire, and he was a very frequent visitor at our house, both on Sunday 'open house' days and at other times when my father, already an established journalist, was helping him with his first book, *The White Peacock*. I first met D.H. Lawrence ('Bert' to his family and friends) when he was sixteen. My father William Hopkin, a manager of local schools, was always very interested in bright children, especially those of local miners who had few opportunities to get out of the pits. Bert was a promising student, too delicate to be a miner and in need of help to be anything else. One day I ran into the living-room from the garden to find a young man standing on a rug before the fire talking to my father. I was introduced to the visitor. Bert shook my hand, staring at me and I at him. His eyes, very blue, intense, had a light behind them like the light behind a microscope – clear, unblinking, seeing everything. I ran from the room and from that young man, tall, lanky, with a shock of reddish hair, a very high collar (these collars were typical of him; his mother had the idea that a high collar would protect his delicate throat), and a few adolescent pimples on a pale face. Those eyes were strangely Lawrence, seeing everything, sorting everything – they were one of the sources of Lawrence's amazing powers of description and especially of his ability to understand women. After I left the room the effect of those eyes, even as a small child, remained with me.

Bert became a regular visitor to the house, and it was there that he was exposed to the theories of politically important people who gathered from time to time in our living-room. My father William was very politically involved, and this involvement was two-fold. The Boer War was taking place at that time and my father was pro-Boer, for he felt that because the Boers had been the first in the country and had created their own land they should be entitled to stay there without interference. The struggle in Africa was between the Boer farmers and settlers and 'imported' miners intent on making fortunes during the gold rush. Without being quite sure what it all meant, the local miners were determined to punish any man who dared to oppose the actions of their mining brothers. Every miner felt that he, ostensibly, had the right to go there and mine whatever and whenever he wished.

Naturally, to be a pro-Boer in Eastwood during this period was heartily disapproved of. The sensibilities of the local miners finally became roused to the point where groups of them threatened to come and break all our windows, at that time a favourite way of showing one's dislike of a neighbour's politics, habits, or dress. One incident stands out vividly in my memory. A group arrived in front of our house armed with sticks and rocks, calling for my father to come out. He spoke quietly to my mother: 'Take Enid upstairs to the Apple Room. You will be safe there.' The Apple Room was dark as the windows were boarded up on the inside to slow the ripening of our winter apples stored on the shelves. I was about three or four years of age; the noise outside was frightening. My mother and I sat on boxes in the semi-darkness, listening to the noise below. I heard my father step out and the angry miners starting to shout. Then Mother and I heard Father's voice – light, happy, and amusing. The crowd started to laugh, voices softening, anger flowing out as humour moved in. 'Tha's areet, Willie!' said someone. There was a shuffling of feet, a dragging of heavy pit boots, a different sort of laughter, and soon it was quiet in the street. We heard a door close. No windows had been broken.

In this time of unrest and political fights for freedom, however, we could not be sure the incident would not be repeated. The miners, poorly paid, working in tunnels of dubious safety, were becoming restive, demanding a better life, higher wages, and my father was supporting their effort. Meetings were held in Nottingham and also in Eastwood, where my father William and others addressed crowds in the market-place in front of the Sun Inn. More and more people gathered at our house, often including Lawrence, who regarded the politicians with amused tolerance. My father was a member of the Fabian Society, a group of idealistic Socialists intent on peaceful reform and recognition of the working-classes, without any form of violence. Phillip Snowden came, a thin man with a sharp, foxy face and staccato manner. Keir Hardie appeared and became a close friend of my father. We also knew Ramsay MacDonald, quiet and blunderingly dreamy, not a man of strong action. Beatrice and Sidney Webb were there, a gently dedicated pair, fuddy-duddy in their habits. No matter where they were, at 9 p.m. sharp Beatrice nudged Sidney and said: 'Dear, it's 9 o'clock.' Conversation ceased abruptly, and they toddled off to bed.

There were many discussions in our living-room. Not only did we entertain the Fabians, but we also supported the women's movement, as my mother, along with Alice Dax, was involved with the suffragists. Alice, new to the town and wife of the chemist, was an active participant, Mother a quiet one. After meetings in the city of Nottingham, dedicated women such as Annie Kenny, Charlotte Despard, Margaret Bondfield, and – once – one of the Pankhursts came home with us to spend the night under my mother's best linen sheets prepared for the occasion. Bert treated the women's movement with a certain amount of mirth. On 'Wet Sundays', days when it was raining too hard for outdoor walks we had 'open house' meetings. Anyone could come and Bert was frequently present. He was fond of my mother, respected my father, but laughed at, perhaps despised, William's political activities. 'You are wasting your time, Willie,' he said quite often. 'All this will come later, social change, why are you spending energy on it now?'

Lawrence was a silent listener or a rather violent speaker. He emphasized statements by hitting the palm of his left hand with his doubled-up right fist. I can still see him sitting by our fire in winter, shoulders hunched, head down, staring. He did not appear to be listening then suddenly he would speak, sometimes to destroy the other speaker. One evening, when the company was largely local, a town official who considered himself an able architect was delivering a lecture. Lawrence listened for a short time, then, glaring at the lecturer, proceeded to tear the poor man's information to shreds and deliver his own – knowledgeable, brilliant. It seemed that the whole room sprang to life; we could feel the vibrations. The victim, at first annoyed and pouting, soon listened attentively. When the oration was over, he confided that from that short lecture he had learned more than during his four years at college. Such tactics, however, did not endear Lawrence to people in general.

On rainless Sundays our family walked long distances over the countryside, and Lawrence sometimes accompanied us. There were many cross-country paths, linking villages by short cuts, or keeping pedestrians off the narrow, twisty roads and the danger of horse-drawn traffic. These paths usually ran alongside the hedges dividing field from field. At each cross-hedge there was a stile to climb over or squeeze through. The bottoms of hedges were usually rich in flowers. My father was on the board of the Royal Society for the Preservation of Rural England and thus volunteered to walk the paths to keep them open. If a field path could be proved not used for a year, the owner of the land had the right to close it to the public – so we walked many miles, often taking with us a friend as verification that the path had been used. When I was a child our travel companion was frequently Harry Dax, husband of Annie, who had a pocket microscope and introduced me to flowers made big so that it was possible to see how they were constructed, to learn about stamens and pollen, and how bees fertilized and helped to produce seeds. On these long walks my father always carried a pocket book of poems. When we stopped to rest he would read to us. The rhythm of words, the songs of the birds, and the music of water running in cool streams are still mixed in my memory.

To Lawrence everything appeared exciting and fascinating, and when he accompanied us on our walks the excitement was transferred to the rest of us. He saw things we failed to see – perhaps that quality in Lawrence was the most important of all. Suddenly small things would become immense, amusing moments hilarious, disasters dreadful. Life was enlarged. That was part of the secret of his art, raising the commonplace into the sublime. I knew most of the local people who would serve as models for his later characters and, lacking Lawrence's view of them, I might have dismissed them as ordinary. Seeing them through the mirror of his books, though, the reflections gave me a fresh realization of their potential. Lawrence saw underneath the personal shell, and seeing, he used it. His love of playing charades, which he did with intensity, indicated this trait – perhaps because the game allowed full use of imagination, character creating and building, without the limitations of a stage.

The country surrounding our small town was peaceful and beautiful. Lawrence has described it endlessly in his books, and it helps to explain his love of England and his almost compulsive returns there. From the houses and short side streets one stepped immediately into meadows, defined by hedgerows, often crossed by small streams. Because of this the sound of water was never far away. There were woods, smaller groups of trees, hidden ferns, and many flowers in the spring. Clusters of farm buildings were never far away and cattle and horses grazed happily in lush grass. There are wonderful memories of days spent in and out of barns and sheds, watching baby pigs or tenderly handling newly hatched chickens. On warm summer days we children played in the hay, spirits high from the rich, almost aromatic smell of drying grass and flowers, riding on the hay wagons, perched precariously on top of the load, smelling the sweet-herb aroma of horses. The farm kitchens had their own fascination, rich in the smells of fresh-baked bread and the peculiar odour of milk. Since our mothers baked all the bread we ate, all our houses had the same rich yeasty smells on baking days. Our town houses, though, lacked the smells of animals, of manure, of hay. Neither Lawrence's home nor my own had the long low kitchen with a flagstone floor and geraniums blooming in the deep-set window frames that typified many English farmhouses.

Northern England in the spring had other beauties. After the snows, frosts, and winter storms of wind and rain were over, the softer rains of March and April brought flowers, masses of flowers, and bird song. We searched the hedgerows for the first wild violets, white ones or blue or a pale lilac colour. All were scented and the soft perfume told us where to find them. Hedges were usually hawthorn or wild roses, both very fragrant. Honeysuckle added a stronger fragrance. Delicate primroses and cowslips sweetened the air. Many of the woods were carpeted with bluebells, heavily scented. We walked along the slender paths, taking deep breaths and gathering bunches of the slender blossoms to carry home, to recapture the beauty of the woods in our rooms. The English spring was also gloriously musical with the songs of hundreds of birds. Before the other birds were ready the thrush sang at dawn, a lovely fluid song floating in the chill air. The rich throatiness of the blackbird soon joined a contralto to the high notes of the thrush. Finches, hedge sparrows, and many other small birds added sweetness or sadness or gaiety. There were also the meadowlarks, mere spots of brown with gold breasts pouring out their salutation high in the pale spring skies.

Many small towns and even quite diminutive villages used to be, and sometimes still are, dominated by a large house set in its own grounds. Some of these commodious homes were quite old and for the most part they were occupied by well-to-do families who kept a watchful eye on the doings in the village and on its people. Eastwood Hall, according to my memory, was mid-Victorian in style. It differed from similar houses in surrounding villages by the fact that it was unoccupied. The owners rarely visited, but my father knew the family and possessed a key to the large front gates. Since we had right of entry to the grounds we spent many happy hours in the meadows, gardens, and small woods surrounding the property. The house itself offered a mystery and many were the tales I invented around it. Everything about the building was neat and tidy yet everything seemed to be wearing a shroud. If one dared to mount the terrace and peep through gaps in the heavily-curtained windows, one saw fascinating yet nameless furniture covered with large white dust sheets exactly as if shrouded from life.

Across a trimly kept lawn in front of the house was an ornamental pond with an island in the centre. The pond and the island had been commandeered by interesting groups of water birds who gave a sense of life to the quiet surroundings. High fences and walls with carefully locked gates protected the property. At the back of the house and well to the rear were stables, a coach house, and very elaborately laid out gardens with greenhouses in which were grown fruits and plants at that time known as 'tropical'. In late summer there were fresh tomatoes, shining and resplendent in their flawless growth. Also clambering round the large glass frames were grape vines, from which in the autumn dangled fascinating and luscious bunches of grapes, such as were known only to the rich.

A gardener lived in a small house that formed an entrance to these marvellous gardens, he and his family acting as guardians of the rear of the property. In late summer and in autumn I was sent with my basket down a side lane to the gardener's cottage, given right of entry and power to buy those shining flawless tomatoes and fascinating grapes. On the south-facing wall, espaliered to catch every gleam of England's reluctant sun, fruit trees produced pears and apples, carefully tended to a perfection rarely seen in our own country gardens.

With the key giving us right of entry to the meadows and streams in the walled property and our permit to purchase the exotic fruits and vegetables, we did indeed lead king-like existences. Frequently Lawrence would walk with us in the park across a stream separating the pasture-type land from that reserved for use by the family should it ever live in the large house. I never knew the history of the shrouded mansion but very frequently we walked in the storyland atmosphere of the shrouds. Lawrence, accompanying me, used that setting for at least one of his novels. In fact I feel that parts of his most recently discovered novel, *Mr Noon*, concerned some of Lawrence's fascination with the story of the house and the deathlike emptiness of the carefully tended house and grounds.

The fields, farms, and woods that we walked in around Eastwood told of the old rural England. The results of the Industrial Revolution were everywhere, but in those Midland districts they were still partly hidden. Walking across the calm countryside and rounding a small hill, the chuff-chuff of the pit engine and bump-bang of shunting railway trucks in the valley below was a surprising intrusion and there, on the other side of the hill, one would see a mine, busy, squalid, and yet with its own stark beauty. I never knew why there was a beauty in the hideous mine buildings. Did it lie in the cold utility? In the hard thrust of machinery into the tranquil day? There is no way to convey Lawrence's horror at this industrial intrusion. Everything about the old mines was dirty, ugly, and oily, from the mountain of waste to the crude overhead stacking and the noise of the engines and trucks – they grew in the fields like dirty mushrooms, always there, the town's livelihood yet an unspoken threat.

The men who worked in the mines were the major link between the mines and the rest of us. When their shift was over the men would swing up in the cage lift to the pit-head, filthy with coal dust, streaked round the eyes and mouth. There were no pit-head baths. The men shuffled home to bathe in a tub of water heated on the kitchen stove, their backs washed by their wives in a ritual that was part of daily mining routine. After their bodies had been cleansed of blackness, the men would eat supper and then leave for the pubs, to meet again their underground companions. Wherever miners were together one was conscious of this strange communication. Speech, if any, was low-toned and usually in the local dialect. There was a communion from man to man, born in the deep dark mine, where danger was always present and each depended on his friend. The mines were a secret world, inhabited by a different race of human beings. Deep in the dark mines the men knew one another with a deep knowledge, almost primitive, animal-like. There was a physical dependence, from each to the other and from all to the pit ponies. Into this communion no one outside could penetrate. The miners were different from us, and we knew it. Their relationships with their wives must have been strange too. Men and women were rarely seen together after work, perhaps because the women were tied to houses by children, or did they realize the mine-born differences and leave the men alone? Was there tenderness? Could there be companionship? Who knows? Even on Sundays there was separation in most cases. The children went to Sunday School, miserable in 'best' clothes and tight new shoes; the women dressed up and went to chapel. Very occasionally a family went to church together. But the men were usually separate. Washed and in their best trousers, they wandered into town, sitting on their haunches in silent communion. Or some wandered off to the little common gardens to work on and with the earth, instead of in it. Women had their own sense of communion and mutual support. In times of trouble, such as a death in the mine, the women rushed to help and comfort one another.

The humanity of men was destroyed during the day by their industry. Mornings were very different. Because the mines were often a long distance from their homes, and since there was no other form of transportation provided, the men had to walk. My family lived in a house that was at a corner of a short-cut to one of the mines. In the very early dawns, before daylight, I often awakened to hear the trudge, trudge of miners taking the path to the mine for the early shift. Sometimes they sang, usually part-songs, the voices beautiful with an underlying rhythm of slud-crunch-slush of the heavy mine boots that were almost dragged along the path. The rhythm spoke of hard, grinding work in the mines, but the music told of the rich companionship of men sharing that labour. The voices stopped, rough talk and laughter followed, soon to return to song, the music fading and blending in the not-quite-daylight air, into the dark blue and soft green lights streaking the before-dawn sky.

Lawrence grew up exposed to this mining ritual. But as it became obvious that he could not follow the occupation of his father he started a dual existence, where he was an observer and recorder of the mining world while he himself moved into the arena of art and letters. Vividly aware of the old England and the mining life, he was destined to drift away, no longer accepted by, or really belonging to, either world. While he had by necessity left his father's occupation, the world of art and letters did not welcome the son of a miner. In Eastwood, too, you either belonged or you didn't. Religion, for instance, was an inherited virtue with the same inevitability as one's job. If the father was a miner, the son was. Lawrence was an exception. This was another factor bringing criticism from the provincial society in which he was raised.

The town's limitations and restrictions were the sources of

Lawrence's struggles for freedom, as expressed in his books. To understand what Lawrence was coping with, it is necessary to give a few examples from my own experience about the kind of community in which we both lived. It was the nature of the time to deny the existence of things that were not understood or were disapproved of. That was the cause of a good deal of the secrecy of the time. When children entered a room where adults were conversing, the conversation immediately shifted. Children knew this, of course, but did not question it, for they quickly learned that there was no answer. The standard reply by adults was: 'When you get older, dear, you will understand.' But somehow one was never old enough.

Such 'rights' as did exist were for adults only. Children, during the Victorian period and on into the early twentieth century, were to be seen and not heard. Boys were expected to be strong, fearless, and tearless, with no expressed emotions; girls to be pure, ignorant, feminine, content with marriage (but unprepared for it), and with no interests outside the home. Class distinctions were insurmountable, and for a child growing up at this time life could be narrow, puzzling, and often lonely. Most natural desires were considered sinful, and the inquiring mind was discouraged and squashed. Childhood fears were many, unresolved, and never explained away. It was a time of innocence, ignorance, and scraps of faulty knowledge gained under cover.

Such imposed limitations and restrictions were often destructive for a child and extremely hurtful. They were illustrated even in the way the houses of the town were arranged. At the end of our garden, for example, was a very high fence, impossible to see over or through, and beyond this fence, the backs of the houses and shops of the main street kept their secret lives. Also beyond that fence, unknown to me, were the secrets of the butcher's shop. Clues came in the terrible screams of agony that drifted over the fence. The harrowing squeals bothered me: someone or something was being hurt. I asked my father, but his explanation was not very helpful. Pigs squealed at the slightest thing, so perhaps one of the species did not like its house, or was hungry. Then he added that I must never go behind the fence to the butcher's shop. One day as I was walking down the main street, the familiar squeals and screams could be heard. I forgot my promise and sneaked in the butcher shop entry, hiding behind boxes. What I saw was horrifying. A large pig hung from a cross-bar by its hind feet, its head near the ground. There was a deep slash in its throat, and two men were squeezing blood from the opening. The animal was still alive, its blood running into a large tin pan. For a moment I was frozen, unable to take my eyes from this grisly scene. Then I turned to run. The two men were so absorbed in getting the last drop of blood that they did not see me. I ran and ran, tears choking me, until I was home, and there vomited all over myself. Mother came rushing: 'Alice, put the kettle on for hot water. Enid has had another sick attack.'

Child to child relationships, friends to confide in, were also limited by class restrictions. Children played with others in their own class and to step out of any ascribed class line could be disastrous. The mining children and the town children did not play together, though we met in school. Father had none of this sense of class distinction, but in Mother it was strong. I began playing with a little girl, Ethel, a miner's daughter. Father was in favour of the friendship, but mother was doubtful. One day, after a session of playing with Ethel, I returned home and described something as 'mucky'. Now 'mucky' was quite a good old word but not one used in refined society. Mother was shocked – where had I heard that word? I said that my friend Ethel used it. It was a 'bad' word, I was told, and I must never play with Ethel again. Pleadings had no effect – and I was heartbroken for months.

Close human friendship being eliminated by force, I turned to imaginary friends. Earlier I had heard Mother and Father speaking of America. The word meant nothing, but they mentioned the dollar. That struck me as a lovely name, probably the name of some little girl. 'Dollar' and I became inseparable friends, long and stumbling conversations took place, and always she was the one of the pair of us who had done the evil deed if a crime was committed. I found another companion under one of the gooseberry bushes in our garden in a large smooth rock, too heavy to lift but fascinating. From the bedroom window I could see the bush and knew of the rock lying there. Gradually the rock became alive at night. After I was forbidden to play with Ethel, 'he' became in my imagination a little man named Tom Tidler. Dollar died a natural death and Tom took her place: from my bed Tom and I played together. I built him a house out of a packing case, furnishing it with dolls' furniture. Every evening at supper I hid food in my clothing and took it out to the little house, leaving it on the table. I told my father about Tom. He was wise enough to know and understand my loneliness; he left Tom with me. Every morning for as long as Tom 'lived' the stolen food was removed from the table. For some reason we never told my mother about Tom.

Dollar and Tom filled a deep need created in me by the class distinction. As I grew up, real people would come to be substituted. When Bert became my friend I told him about Tom Tidler. Bert accepted Tom quite seriously, but said: 'You know, Enid, Tom will go away one day soon, but you must not mind; there will be someone else.' This incident underlines a difference between my father and Lawrence. My father took Tom Tidler seriously and removed the food in order to maintain my illusion; Lawrence also accepted Tom Tidler, for the moment, but with an eye for the future.

In my childhood moral values were tight. One did or did not do or say certain things. I was strictly brought up always to tell the truth. Excuses and lying were not permitted. On the other hand, in my parents' home there was some understanding of the difference between lying and imagination. I had an aunt who never made allowances for imagination, which is part of the gift of story-telling. To Aunt Bessie's way of thinking something you imagine, however outlandish or vivid, was a lie and you were whipped for it. My parents understood the difference, although I knew that my father's recognition of it was a little wider than my mother's. But fortunately for me they complemented each other so that my flights of fancy were never punished.

Aunt Bessie had two children, both girls. The older one was stuffy and full of diseases, either imagined or real. It was dangerous to ask her how she was. She told you in great detail. 'I don't enjoy very good health' was one of her favourite remarks, leaving you with the impression she really *enjoyed* very poor health, since it gave her a sense of notoriety and separated her from the common herd. Her name was also Bessie, and she was distinguished from her mother by being called 'Little Bessie'. The younger child was far more approachable, occasionally even willing to get her shoes and her dress dirty when with such a ruffian as their cousin Enid, and in spite of the fact that dirt almost always ended in a whipping for poor Gracie. I was exempt from the whippings because I was someone else's child, although I never escaped the lectures.

On one occasion when Little Bessie's notoriety through illness was raised to incredible heights I felt that I, also, must have something of equal importance. So I described in minute detail all

19

my dolls, ones I did not own. The other girls were very impressed. Aunt Bessie, being very indignant when Mother came to pick me up, let Mother 'have it'. 'How could I be allowed to have all those dolls?' Mother immediately corrected it – I had two only – one a baby doll dressed in my own christening clothes hidden away in a dresser, and a golliwog. The others were all in my imagination. Aunt Bessie was horrified. 'If she was my child I would thrash her within an inch of her life,' said my gentle aunt. Fortunately Mother understood, though she did tell me that it was both rude and unkind to use imagination in order to make myself bigger and better than another person. In this way being or not being a liar was a complicated business.

On our way to and from school our three-mile walk passed over two canal bridges. When it was necessary to pass a special pipeline over the canals there was no way of incorporating the line, so it had to pass alongside the existing bridge. In the case of one bridge the pipe was very high above the water, and the water itself was very deep. The pipe offered great temptation for daring children to walk across from one side of the canal to the other. Naturally this was forbidden by parents and authorities. Naturally we all stopped when we approached the bridge, laughing and daring one another to pipe across. Then one day one of the boys with whom I was in competition for deeds of derring-do, dared me to cross. Perhaps, fortunately, some instinct warned me not to do it, but expanding his chest and giving me a withering look he started on his journey. I saw how perilous it was, and was thankful I had not accepted the challenge. We all ran to the other side of the bridge to watch the passage. My competitor made it across but I noticed his face was a greenish-white and I saw he needed some sort of support. Moving to stand near him, I joined in the congratulations offered by the other children. I also noticed that he was shaking all over and quite unable to control the trembles, so I stayed close to him. I knew his parents and that if ever they found out about the exploit he would be very severely punished. He gave me a very strange look of understanding and gratitude for my support, but we said nothing as we left the scene and continued our way to our homes.

That was not the end of the story. Apparently someone had seen us congregating at the bridge and he or she told my parents that I had crossed the pipe-line. Knowing my taste for adventure, in spite of my denials and those of the other children, the adult was believed and I was not. After all, no children could be believed as they would support me in my lie. I was severely punished and Mother's nagging assumed, I realized later, a form of cruelty that became intolerable. She knew now that she could never trust me again, that I would continue lying to support my own stories. Finally I could take it no longer. It was a courage I lacked. I decided to admit that I lied, taking the second punishment which would be even more severe in the hope that would clear matters up and take Mother 'off my back'. That was what happened, but it did not remove the weight of Mother's judgement. Those were heavy days and finally I could not take it alone, so I told my father the story. My father understood and I'm sure he believed me, but he was never critical of Mother's judgement. Instead he pointed out where I had been wrong. If you, yourself, know that your story is true, you must honour it no matter what happens. You must never let down truth by another lie in order to seemingly make things easier for yourself. When I asked him should I tell Mother about the second lie he said: 'No, you must learn by it and develop courage along with truth.'

For reasons still unknown to me, I never told Bert of this incident in my life. I knew of his love and admiration for my mother and I felt instinctively that she had been wrong, but revelation of her wrongdoing might upset our family relationships.

The town's thinking was so restrictive that it even affected things as small as household decoration, such as the kind of curtains one hung at one's window. Almost every house in Eastwood had lace curtains at the windows. These were made in the nearby town of Nottingham, so to hang them at your windows was to support local economy, and to reject them made one a bit of a traitor. The curtains were a big responsibility in a town where coal dust begrimed the buildings, and dirty curtains were a disgrace. One knew the sort of woman who lived in this or that house by the state of her curtains. Keeping them clean was a major operation. Most curtains were looped back at the bottom, the loops held in place by ribbons or velvet bands. Frequently they were attractive, but one tired of the inevitability. Washing them was an all-day job, having to be done by hand and with great care. Removed from the windows, they were carefully shaken then put to soak. They were dried full length on the clothes lines and, when almost dry, were removed and stretched from end to end by two people working in a rhythm of careful pull and release tension. After all this the curtains were re-hung, unless they required light pressing with a warm iron. Mother was beginning to question whether all this labour was worthwhile.

Alice Dax became firm friends with my mother soon after she moved to Eastwood. She did not approve of lace curtains but instead hung casement drapes at her windows. These were of an unpatterned coloured material, strange and distinguished – and appeared in a lace-curtain-bound area. That was fine for Alice, as the Dax living quarters were behind and above the chemist shop, where windows were not readily seen. Mother liked Alice's idea and many yards of material were purchased and made up. Soon our big bay window gleamed with a soft golden light through the new straight-hanging curtains. I thought they were beautiful. Local people, however, had no ideas of beauty: we were defying established convention as well as the economy. Again the townspeople threatened to smash our windows, but reconsidered when they remembered that William was chairman of the County Council and very popular in town.

Physically the small town of Eastwood, rarely free from coal dust, was dirty and ugly. Out of the shabby, often grimy houses, however, emerged dedication, courage, ideas, fights for freedom, self-education, music and drama. Mother and Alice were leaders in a literary society where we selected books and read them aloud. Alice formed a drama group with my parents' assistance; our thespian abilities were never outstanding, but the attempts were fun. We learned to conquer stage fright, as pretending to be someone else was a great relief. Soon I started writing my own plays and dragging playmates in as performers, family and other adults as the audience. In the early days of the town's awakening travelling players visited. They were amazing – dramatic, often tragic, and concerned with the triumph of virtue over sin. Generally the 'good' man won and secured the girl if she had not already been killed in the tragic parts. These plays were performed in any shed available, curtains occasionally rising at the wrong moment to reveal a partially dressed heroine. Or stockings, corsets, and wigs would mysteriously disappear, to be found in the front rows of the audience, having fallen ignominiously from under the curtain. There were no dressing rooms.

Early attempts at local drama had also included the mummers. They performed plays during the Christmas season, going from house to house, offering to give performances before the assembled family. Father always invited them in and we listened with rapt attention. Sometimes the recital was in the local dialect, not too easy to understand, but the acting was often superb. When the plays were over the performers were fed Christmas fare and sent away with a little money. The travelling players ceased to visit in the early part of the century, but the mummers were with us until the First World War.

Eastwood had a Mechanics' Library that opened every Thursday evening, when one would stagger under a load of books already read to exchange them for new stimulating stories. Local taste was to an extent guided by the librarian. There was little chance that one might get hold of the 'wrong' books. My tastes ran to Jules Verne for adventure, and to Dickens and Scott. Once I did pick up a novel that was considered 'not quite nice'. The librarian made no comment, but my parents were at once informed. The book disappeared from my room.

In Eastwood, churches were strong and socially orientated. The Anglican congregation looked down long noses at the Congregationalists, who in turn felt superior to the Methodists. The Baptists seemed to be at the bottom of the social ladder. Climbing from one church to a higher group was difficult: either you belonged or you didn't. The Masons flourished in the town, usually holding evening meetings in the Mechanics' Institute.

During my early childhood my father was deeply absorbed by various aspects of the Church. As a leader in the Sunday School division and as a lay preacher he knew all the grand old hymns still sung in those far away days.

Lawrence wrote a short story that he called 'Hymns in a Man's Life'. It was a good story and impressed me very much. My appreciation of it has continued, realizing as the years pass that hymns have had their own tremendous importance in the life of this child, and that I, too, must some day write a chapter to be called 'Hymns in a Child's Life'. On Sunday evenings we often had musical sessions. One of my aunts was a violinist. She had a friend who was a skilled pianist, and that friend knew a man who played the flute, so we had an orchestra. For several hours on chosen Sundays we played and sang the old folk-songs of England, Ireland, and Scotland, and above all we exercised our lungs on those good old hymns. As a result of those Sunday evening gatherings, at a very early age I knew and could sing most of the great hymns. It is perhaps necessary to admit that my knowledge and execution of these things was not based solely on piety. The hymns themselves and my singing were a form of freedom in a child's world. I could sing my heart out with joy and with the knowledge that no one could reprimand me for over-loud singing, because if they did they would be criticizing my expression of religion.

For some reason I could not then explain, I liked best the strong, almost violent hymns. Through them I was expressing my own intense joy in a freedom with which no one dared interfere. I am not suggesting that this gain of freedom was the main reason for loving the hymns, as even at this early age I was developing my own sense of spiritual need. I lived in a culture where we were constantly warned that God would punish each of our little misdeeds. Through the singing I could forget the notion that God would be waiting to deal with me for each of my wrongdoings. At that time it was wonderful for me that I could sing about a God who was beyond mere punishing for trivialities and move into a world of pure, spiritual joy. Through the hymns I developed a feeling of God's greatness, a sense of something beyond crime and punishment, something removed from, even though it was a part of, the narrow world in which I lived.

In those early days I briefly had a friend from Germany, and we sang and talked about hymns in my language and in his. Occasionally a hymn sounded better in German with seemingly greater force in the words, and for some reason 'A Mighty Fortress is our God' had more splendour and more meaning when my friend sang 'Ein feste Burg ist unser Gott'. In our way we were emphasizing the cultural weight given to spirit by sound and words.

I well remember just a hint of wickedness when my German friend and I agreed to sing the hymns each in his own language. We wanted to know how it would sound. It was noticed by some members of the congregation with amusement and smiles, but by others with annoyance, but it could have been a very good lesson for the Church at that moment. I'm afraid, however, that they did not appreciate it.

In this manner the hymns of my childhood were important to me. They expressed a craving for pure freedom limited only by my developing spiritual growth and the beauty and power of the old hymns of faith. Somehow God seemed very much nearer as I knew he was aware of me, a child seeking joy in a crumbling world.

On Saturdays the Salvation Army played at street corners – harrowing, out-of-tune hymns, accompanied by a bonneted lady with a tambourine, and a doleful trumpet and drum. The few stragglers who stopped joined in the singing. It was really rather awful but warm and 'saving'. The Army was after all of our souls, and our money in the collection: the tambourine served the double purpose of rhythm and gathering the offerings. I was not permitted to join the devout circle around the Army, but occasionally I did, enjoying the 'service' far more than that of the church we attended. From the Army one could escape if and when it became boring.

The town of Eastwood was physically ugly; one long main road wound a curving way from south to north. There were so many shops, small crowded places, many selling the same goods. Buildings were generally red brick with blue-grey slate roofs. There were few new structures and age had mellowed the starkness of most. Here and there better-class houses rubbed shoulders with the small shops. A number of pubs were evident, noisy and smelling of beer and tobacco. At night, though, when so many cultural events took place, the town became magic, especially through the eyes of a child. At dusk the lamplighter appeared with his long pole, a light at the end. Quickly he walked from standard to standard, turning on the gas and lighting the lamps with his pole. If I could escape from the house I would follow him a little way, enjoying standing in the freshly made pools of light, terrified in the gloom between the lamps. On foggy nights the light was diffuse, diminished, forming rainbows. It was so beautiful. I followed the lamplighter as far as I dared, racing from lamp to lamp on the return home, afraid of what lurked in the dark places between the lights.

My parents and Alice Dax were at the centre of change and culture in Eastwood, and D.H. Lawrence turned to them for cultural opportunities – until later, when he went far beyond and they turned to him. His visits to our family naturally became more rare as his own opportunities and experiences expanded. His quick wit had earned him a scholarship to grammar school in Nottingham, and following graduation he was given scholarships to Nottingham University and Ilkeston teachers' training college. Lawrence never returned physically to the mining influence; he remained withdrawn and more or less 'classless' all his life. However, almost all of his earlier work was centred around and drawn from his earlier mining influences and contacts. And there, of course, the trouble began, because people identified themselves in his characters and were infuriated.

During this period I was having fairly frequent attacks which had been thought to result from nervous tension, or apprehension. All at once the nature of these attacks changed, becoming violent pains which the local doctor diagnosed as intestinal ulceration. I was put on a limited diet, but soon I had a particularly violent attack and a specialist was called from the city. His diagnosis of appendicitis was immediate, but too late – the thing had ruptured and peritonitis developed. At this time appendicitis was almost unknown in country areas. I could not be moved so the big bedroom of our home was stripped and converted into a hospital ward. Two nurses were obtained and the operation took place there. On completion of the operation the surgeon left, taking his nurses with him, while for three or four nights the local doctor moved into the house to see me through the dark hours, so that mother could sleep. During the long months of recovery Lawrence visited me whenever he was in town, and we played games. One of our favourites was Snakes and Ladders. For Lawrence the game was exciting: it was a triumph to go up a ladder and total, world-shaking disaster to be swallowed by a snake. We yelled with joy or almost wept in exasperation. This was exactly the medicine I needed for dull days, often dreary and pain-filled. As soon as I was promoted to a bath chair (that forerunner of the modern wheelchair) Lawrence took me for walks, pushing the chair. We found flowers, gay pebbles, and skeleton leaves in the most unlikely places.

No matter what he was doing – lecturing on architecture, teasing my father about his political activities, planning charades, walking in the country, or playing games with a sick child – Lawrence made moments golden, enhanced and raised them to their limits, causing life to assume a splendour. In my early adolescence, when life was so horribly restricted and I wasn't allowed to do or say anything without my mother's surveillance, Lawrence was inevitably aware of the hold Mother had on me and its potential effects on my future. One day he said to her: 'Sallie, you must free Enid. You are giving her a cloistered soul and it is not good. She has to go out on her own, make her own decisions, her own mistakes, and find herself in a changing world. You cannot do it for her.' This talk worried me a great deal. What was a 'cloistered soul'? Was it some sort of strange illness and, if so, why was Bert blaming Mother for it? However, Lawrence's own Puritan soul kept him from determining how much freedom I should really be granted.

Lawrence's relationships with women began, as do all men's, with his mother. In Lawrence's case, the mother–son relationship was intense, because of his frailty and repeated illnesses when his mother was the only nurse. My father's first meeting with Lawrence illustrates this. He met Mrs Lawrence on the street when she was pushing a perambulator, and he asked about the new baby. Mrs Lawrence pulled back the covers to show a tiny fragile infant, white as his pillow. William said to himself: 'That child cannot live.' But Lawrence did live: always delicate, he tended to play and walk with girls. The bigger, robust boys gave him an unhappy time in school, until he became able to show his mental abilities and intellectual superiority. Lawrence was early a victim of pneumonia. Nursed through this by his mother, the two became very close. In her frail son, Mrs Lawrence found the sort of man she felt she should have married. Not realizing the truth about herself, or the worth of the man she had married, she pushed her husband further and further away, leeching intellectual vitality from Bert. Many of his problems, shown in *Sons and Lovers*, began here. In his later years, Lawrence realized that the relationship with his mother was not all that it seemed to be and also that much of his power and ability came from his father. He regretted his earlier alienation from this man. Lawrence's first book, *The White Peacock*, was placed in his mother's hands as she lay dying, shortly after its publication.

Lawrence began seeing Jessie Chambers when he was aged sixteen, and was a frequent visitor to Haggs Farm, her family home. This was a beautiful setting for a budding romance. On the edge of woods formerly part of Sherwood Forest, the farm was truly rural, removed from contact with the mines and the communal world. This was a wonderful period for Lawrence, as an interim between his mine-influenced childhood and entry into the wider world of letters. He and Jessie worked together, reading good books and helping each other with their homework. Lawrence wanted to go further but Jessie held back, and he realized she was unable to accompany him in his destined direction. His mother had developed a jealousy of Jessie, since the friendship took Lawrence away from home in the evenings. Jessie in turn had her doubts about Mrs Lawrence and she disliked my mother, being aware of my mother's certainty that Jessie would not be Lawrence's permanent woman. Many biographers have had a field day with this relationship. I never knew Jessie very well, as I was just a young girl at the time.

Lawrence often brought his women home to my mother. She evaluated them, and she never cared too much for Jessie, saying: 'That's not your woman.' And, of course, she wasn't. Later he brought Louie Burrows. And even when Lawrence was engaged to Louie, my mother said he would never marry her for it wouldn't work out. Then he came with Alice Dax who was to be Clara in *Sons and Lovers*. Alice was a great friend of my mother's, but in that case she herself knew she wasn't the woman, and more or less terminated the relationship. Alice said she could never live up to what Lawrence wanted, and could never live in the sort of catch-as-catch-can manner that was so necessary to him. Then he brought Frieda to our house. I was away at the time, but my mother told me about Frieda and said that Lawrence was going to marry her. Mother apparently told him that this *was* his woman, and that he would never really be happy with Frieda, but she was the woman that he ought to marry. By not being 'happy', Mother meant that there would be conflict, but that Frieda would be strong enough for Lawrence and would give him the stimulation he needed. Jessie would have been a leaner, eventually, if not in the beginning. But not Frieda. Frieda didn't lean on anyone; she was a most remarkable person.

I remember one night in spring we were at Mountain Cottage near Cromford in Derbyshire, my parents, myself, Lawrence's sister Ada and brother George, and a friend named Arabella York and some friends of mine, when Frieda came in wearing a most extraordinary hat and dress – both of which Lawrence had made for her. He was quite a good seamster and at that time used to trim all her hats and make many of her clothes. Lawrence decided to walk over the hills and asked for volunteers to accompany him. A light rain was falling, so only my father and I, Arabella York and one of my friends decided to brave the weather. It was quite a wonderful walk, with Lawrence as usual elaborating on the beauty of the hills in the misting rain. After our return to the cottage we all had something to eat and then Frieda sat down at the piano with a candle on either side. We all sang English folk-songs and Frieda and Lawrence sang German songs. I sat at the open window. There was a moon, and I can remember so plainly the view down the hillside to the road, the mountains further away and the perfume from the lilies-of-the-valley coming up through the open window. And I remember the group around the piano in the candlelight, Frieda singing with a cigarette hanging out of the corner of her mouth. And Frieda, who was not a good pianist, every now and then would strike wrong notes. After several of these Lawrence would lose his temper and scream at her, Frieda would scream back, and it would be a free-for-all for a moment. The whole scene was very dramatic, as we stood in mid-chorus wondering what would happen next. Suddenly it was all over, and Frieda would settle down and go back to playing, and we would all start to sing again.

The quarrels between Lawrence and Frieda were extremely violent but short-lived. When they were over they finished utterly, leaving no resentment on either side. And they walked together, did things together. In their presence you felt a strange, antagonistic harmony. They would always come clean with each other, emotionally clean, exposing whatever they were feeling. There was little difference between them in rage. They would yell back and forth, especially Lawrence yelling at Frieda, and sometimes she would throw something at him — whatever was handy. If it was a plate that was all right. And I'm sure, if he had *not* had the conflict with Frieda, he would have died sooner.

Lawrence didn't want to have a grand house and the things that went with it. He wanted to be free of things like wall-to-wall carpeting, and he was. So they lived this sort of camping-out existence, and they shared household chores. You see, Lawrence didn't approve of the way Frieda did things. She came from an aristocratic family with masses of servants who did everything for her: her clothes were laid out, her bath was prepared, the nightgown she left on the floor was put away — and so on. When Lawrence married Frieda her clothes were always jumbled together in her chest of drawers and she could never find anything. So he taught her how to divide her clothes — in this drawer you put your underwear, in this one your blouses — Frieda was thrilled by this, thinking of it as a game. It was funny to her. And when she cooked, she always got terribly dirty.

Frieda was never concerned about her appearance, whereas Lawrence was always neat, always immaculate; not always dressed in a tie but personally clean. I don't think he would ever admit that he was socially conscious in that way but he was. He would pour scorn on shows of class superiority on the one hand, but on the other he was subdued by it. He knew and cultivated many of the wealthy and superior in England, and he was always flattered by their attention. Frieda would help to keep people away while Lawrence wrote, but there was no lovey-dovey pampering.

The organization of Lawrence's writing time worked very well until their efforts were jerked out from under them by threats of war in Europe. We had heard rumbles from Europe for quite some time, but we were sure war could not happen and when it did the world was horrified. In England we felt that had the diplomatic Edward VII still been alive he would have somehow ironed things out. In any case we felt it would not last, because England could lick Germany in a few weeks with one hand tied behind her back. But time dragged on and it did last, with not only the Army and Navy involved but the effects of war spreading everywhere. In small towns like our own young men were called up, after a few weeks sending back photographs of themselves in uniform. The next communication was all too often a letter beginning: 'We regret to inform you . . .'.

The war affected my family's fortunes considerably. The miners, egged on by would-be reformers, seethed in unrest, and eventually a long strike developed when nobody worked, nobody bought anything, and businesses suffered – some starved out of existence. My grandfather had a pit boot business in Eastwood; with nobody going down in the mines, pit boots were not needed.

Down Mansfield Road, Grandfather owned a little shoemaking and repair workshop. The building itself was unusual, being part of the wall that surrounded the property of Eastwood Hall. It was a very high wall, and at the point of Grandfather's workshop it bulged to create what must have been at one time a small house.

The main room opened directly on to the footpath, as was so often the case in these small town houses. In this room with his back to the window sat 'Old William', an artist in leather work who was employed by my grandfather to make and repair shoes. On the other side of the room sat Old William's helper, a silent man, friendly in a speechless way, who assisted with the less demanding jobs. The room was never clean. The floor was dirty and covered with leather scraps and unmentionable rubbish. Winter and summer a fire burned merrily in an old cook stove. This stove had two hobs that were always warm. On one of them a kettle bubbled with dancing lid, and under it was the oven. The hob on the other side of the fire covered a tank of water that was permanently hot and on it stood a large teapot in which tea was always brewing.

I loved to run down Mansfield Road and spend some time in the workshop. Some of the greatest moments of my early years were when I watched Old William work and listened to his songs. At one time a sailor in a sailing ship, Old William knew many of the ancient sea shanties and would sing them as he worked. These songs were always accompanied by the swish of linen thread being drawn through beeswax for stitching the best quality shoes and the tap-tap-tap of the assistant's hammer as he nailed the less expensive ones. I sat on a lump of wood on the incredibly dirty floor and was given over-brewed tea in a cracked cup. Since tea at home was forbidden to one so young, I thought that this was delicious.

At that time the town had many men on crutches with deformed feet. This was the result of injuries received when, as child labourers aged six or seven, they were carried to the mines by their fathers to work the low seams where the men could not go. Frequently falls of rock and coal gave the children permanent injuries. When fully grown, the injured man was taken to Old William's workshop, where the old man took the injured foot into his hands, closed his eyes and felt the foot over and over, making a mental picture of the shape of the injury. He then constructed a shoe that fitted perfectly. He had taken no measurements and had no photograph of the foot, just a mental picture to guide him. Perhaps this skill was partly influenced by the fact that William himself was also lame. He had received a bad accident in his seafaring days, leaving him with curiously crossed legs so that he usually walked with two canes but was able to sit comfortably enough on a stool for his work.

William's sea shanties were quite fascinating, not only to me but to my father and D.H. Lawrence as well. Those two men wished to record the songs and the music; in modern times such records would be invaluable. Too often the recording sessions were planned but later abandoned for some reason, possibly because of Lawrence's frequent absences for long periods from town. In the end the recordings were not made, and Old William died with his sea shanties unsung in the modern world. His songs, however, continue as a shadowy memory, accompanied by the swish of linen thread through beeswax and the tap-tap-tap of the hammer, making shoes so perfect that the wearer stepped lightly into his future.

Grandfather's business practically faded away. Suddenly we realized that the town was very dependent on the miners' wages and on their buying power. My mother had established for herself a good business, travelling by bicycle to outlying farms where she exhibited samples of assorted goods which could be ordered from her. At first this was very successful, but the success was short-lived. During a war such a business could no longer exist, to my mother's bitter disappointment. With no money available in their homes, women and children could not buy shoes or clothing. Our only family income came from my father's position as local postmaster and his poorly paid journalism. It was ironic that his work to 'liberate' the workers should rebound against him.

I was very conscious of the family struggles, and decided to leave college and get a job – which I did, to my parents' distress and relief. On one occasion, when I had a day off from my job in the head office of a bank in Nottingham, I was at home, daily chores completed, wondering what to do next. Mother was seated at the kitchen table, head resting in her hands, eyes sunk in a blind misery. This picture became too much for me, and I decided to go to the post office and see if I could help my father as it was the clerk's day off. Arriving at the office I noticed my father's face, haggard and drawn. He asked if my mother was alone in the house, and I said yes. He told me to go back immediately and never to leave my mother alone. If she left the house I was to follow, unseen. Should she attempt anything foolish, since she was really quite ill, I must then shout for help. Terrified by the urgency in William's voice, I rushed home in time to see Mother leave the house, walking up Nottingham Road. On and on she walked, head down, intent in her misery, and I followed, keeping out of sight, up to Hill Top and round the corner towards Moorgreen. Where was she going? The reservoir? What could I do? Would anyone be around to help? Unfalteringly Mother reached the water and stood by the edge. I hid in the bushes, still with a cold fear. Suddenly she moved back, turned and walked through the gates on to the road that led home.

'I have just been out for a walk,' she said, when I came walking in innocently. 'Would you like some tea – and I think there's a piece of leftover cake.'

That's how it was during the war – tension, fears, misery, death all around us, and a sinking feeling that never again would things be the same. The Victorian false security had gone forever. The war that would be over in a week dragged on, changing into 'war to end wars'. All families suffered, even the rich. We took Belgian refugees into our home, rather lazy people who expected to be waited on and cooked for. After war was declared and zeppelins began to arrive I was living and working in London, and Mother felt that I should leave my little apartment in the centre of the city close to my work on Victoria Street, and move to a 'safe' suburb removed from city dangers. I had an aunt and uncle and two cousins who were living in Clapham, and I was told to take up residence with them. They were more than willing to have me as a paying guest, to ease their own difficulties in a war-torn city. What Mother did not know was that Clapham was one of the entry routes for attacks by air and, generally, for the zeppelins. When there was public warning of an approaching air attack my uncle ordered me and his wife and their two children – big boys of about eleven or twelve – to take up residence under the kitchen table, strong, heavy, and well-built. There we remained until the all-clear, but it was far from comfortable, the boys being at the physically active stage when legs and feet in heavy boots constantly wriggled. This situation became too much for me and, since the warnings came mostly at night and any moonlight was obscured by dark drapes on the windows, I found it safe to slip out from under the 'protective' table and sit by the window where I could both hear and, by manipulation of the black curtains, see a little of the action below. The chief danger in those days was not so much from bombs but from flying pieces of shrapnel.

One night, while I was working in Nottingham, a warning came of approaching zeppelins. Everything came to a standstill, and people were ordered to stay where they were or seek cover in cellars. I immediately thought of my parents and especially my mother, making herself ill through worry. I decided that somehow I must get home. There was no legitimate way out of the building, but I remembered that coal for heating had been delivered that day through the coal chute. Employees were already in the basement so unseen I slipped around the corner. Finding the pile of coal I climbed up to the chute, lifted the lid and escaped.

The whole town was very silent, very dark, and I can still hear the tread-tread-tread of the bobbies walking the street. All my attention was on listening so that I could find a place to hide if the treading should come my way. Even the sudden appearance of a cat was terrifying in the dark. It doesn't take too much to rouse one's imagination in this situation: there was no traffic, and no light anywhere. Gaining the country roads I felt safer, but this was short-lived. Suddenly there was a thunderous explosion as a bomb hit the ironworks in the valley not far from my home town. My attention was directed to the sky above me and there I saw moving, in the direction of Sheffield, an object that in its passage resembled a fat pencil. It was immediately overhead, travelling fast, and I knew it must be a zeppelin. For a moment I panicked and jumped into the roadside ditch, then realized that from up there I would be invisible or just a spot on the road below, unworthy of a bomb. So I continued on my way, later to meet my parents coming towards me, hoping to find me in the town.

No one was safe anywhere. It was the beginning of the Great Fear, the end of all forms of security all over the world – the end of privacy, of the right to one's own life – if that had indeed ever existed. The Lawrences were in England when the war was declared and were not allowed to return to Europe because of the war. The fact that Frieda was German added to the general tensions from which we all suffered. Lawrence was physically unfit for trench warfare, but even so had to go in regularly for physical examinations. This was a torture to him, being obliged to stand or sit naked with many other men and sometimes female nurses for long periods of time in long waiting lines. This was all unnecessary because it was already established that his illness, tuberculosis, was beyond any hope of relief or cure. There was little chance of selling his manuscripts or short stories, and Lawrence and Frieda suffered from extreme poverty, often dependent on friends for food or a place to live.

A form of continual harassment seemed to follow them wherever they went, even into a tiny stone cottage that was on a farm on the Cornish coast. There was no electricity or plumbing and water had to be carried in pails from a nearby spring. There was a privy at the bottom of the garden. At night this posed problems, and it was necessary to take either candles or a flashlight. Local people, who were almost all suspicious of strangers and aware that Frieda was German, reported to the police that the couple were signalling to U-boats out on the ocean. Since the flashlight was necessary merely to find their way to the privy, the whole incident was quite hilarious – but not to Lawrence.

Following the report to the police, officers raided the cottage and, finding flower plans sketched by Lawrence in the days of his botanical studies, confiscated them as 'shipping and battle details made by the Lawrences'. The local police had no idea that a flower would have a detailed 'plan', so assumed that Lawrence's flower sketches were made for subversive reasons. These sketches were sent to headquarters in London as proof positive of evil actions. Fortunately the London police were better informed botanically, and the error was exposed. These unfortunate incidents, however, were regarded as peace disturbances, and the Lawrences were ordered to leave the area and not to move anywhere near to the ocean. Such incidents, together with condemnation of his books, were largely responsible for Lawrence's later rejection of his beloved England and his encroaching bitterness. Such harassment was widespread, not only from government acts but in everyday encounters such as the distribution of white feathers by 'well-meaning', patriotic ladies to healthy-looking young men not in uniform, as a way to indicate to the world that these men were cowards. They would walk up to a young man on the street, pin the feather to his shoulder or back, announcing to the public that he was unwilling to go to fight. These women had no prior knowledge of their victims and Lawrence – tall and appearing healthy – was presented with such a white feather one day while walking in London. This was just one more humiliation leading him to decide, after the war, that he would leave England and would never return.

At last the war to end wars came to an end, its dream of being the last war still part of a world expectation, but, as we have later learned, that dream had no reality. An exhausted Europe and a triumphant America, together with a disillusioned England, celebrated the end of hostilities. We danced and yelled in Piccadilly. The British let down their guard and did things previously unacceptable by British standards. This type of celebration was natural since war itself loosens an abomination over the whole world. Gradually things settled down, but never again to what had been considered normal.

The Lawrences, who had suffered so much pain, humiliation, and condemnation at the hands of England, which Lawrence himself had so dearly loved, left that country in anger, declaring

they would never return. I was then working with the National
Institute of Agricultural Botany in Cambridge. In 1921 I married
and a new dimension was added to my life. The man I married was
Laurence E. Hilton, a man born in London and a resident of that
city. In spite of several scholarships awarded to help him through
his studies for the medical profession, he was forced into the civil
service (a nice safe job with a pension) by autocratic parents. He
greatly disliked his civil service job but was open as a happy
partner to my future explorations.

In 1922 my mother died after a somewhat bitter illness, bitter
because she had been an intense woman who loved life, and to the
horror of people with her at the time of her end, she looked at each
one of us and said, 'Can't any of you help me? I don't want to die, I
have so much left to do.' Of course we could not, but the things
she had not accomplished were left with us in a burden of grief and
perhaps a new understanding of the limits imposed on life.

When Lawrence heard of her death he was abroad but
immediately wrote my father an extraordinary and unforgettable
letter that added to grief yet soothed the loss:

I learned this minute from Ada about Sallie. But I knew Sallie
was turning away to go. And what can one do? But it hurts, the
inevitable hurt, our life coming to an end. But Sallie had a fine
adventurous life of the spirit, a fine adventurous life, and it's the
adventure that counts, not the success. If she was tired now, at
least it was after a vivid travel with you; you travelled a fine
adventurous way together. And if the arriving is in a waste
place, what does it matter? You made a long trek, like pioneers,
and you led me over some frontiers as well. And if Sallie had to
go to sleep, being really tired, having gone a long way for a
woman, and if you or I have to go on over queer places further,

well the rest of the journey she goes with us like a passenger now, instead of a straining traveller. But one has got to live. Here on this high desert it seems so remote and so near to Devonshire Drive. There will be another grave in that cemetery now, down Church Street. It makes me feel I'm growing old. Never mind. One must strike camp and pack up the things and go on.

With love that belongs to the old life.

D.H. Lawrence

At this time Lawrence's words to me as a little girl in my home reminding me of the great big beautiful world outside my window, and urging me to go and see it, were gnawing at my own curiosity about that world and stimulating a desire to begin the exploration and so satisfy the deep needs of a roving mind. The Lawrences had always urged my parents to visit them in places where they had stayed, even briefly. They had received letters saying: 'William, you and Sallie must come here and see and feel the beauty of this place,' but there was never quite enough money or time. Incidentally almost all Lawrence's letters to my parents ended with the phrase: 'Give my regards to that haughty Enid.' So I persuaded my slightly timid husband to begin the exploration, and thus started a new and endlessly fascinating way of life bounded only by our individual jobs and time limits.

I so well remember plans for our first trip abroad. I had told Bert that my husband and I were contemplating travel, and he told us the best and cheapest way to travel, which he certainly knew from his own experiences . . . but my husband had his own ideas. He heard from talk in his government office of a ship, I think the Cunard line, leaving London for India and destined to pause at several Mediterranean ports on its trip through that ocean. He thought it might be a good idea to explore Europe from the safety of an ocean liner. Apparently other people had the same idea and there were two large groups of Americans on board. Each section of the American groups represented some club, of which I had at that time no knowledge. So we embarked, had some rough weather through the Bay of Biscay, but by the time we reached Gibraltar the days were perfect. There the boat remained two or three days, and we and many others landed and explored and discovered a love for that part of southern Spain. Then we re-embarked but the ship was delayed overnight while ship's officers armed with stretchers searched the city and bars and brothels for missing passengers. Some, drunk, were carried aboard on the stretchers, not to reappear at the meal tables or walking the decks for a discreet period of time. I was still rather innocent and did not understand it.

At the next port of call, Marseilles, the same thing happened, and again at Toulon. Marseilles for us was too large, too commercial, and too military, with noisy soldiers pushing at one another in the streets and making flippant remarks in their native tongue at any passing woman. Toulon was beautiful to my exploring eyes. We anchored in the bay and boarded launches to be taken to town. I still see that little water trip to the city. The harbour was large and filled with many kinds of boats. We landed at the quay which ran along the front of the city, next to a road, with rows of brightly painted houses several storeys high beyond it, with occasional gaps where mysterious narrow roads opened into small tree-filled squares with often a fountain in the centre. I still have wonderful memories of Toulon to which we returned several times. I do remember also that 'stretcher' victims from that city delayed the ship longer than they had done earlier. From later visits it was easy to understand why, with the difficulty of recovering inebriated passengers from that labyrinth of painted houses and hotels, on often sinister-looking side streets. There were, I think, two other short stops when our ship remained out in the roads, no passenger leaving.

Then on to Naples. We both remarked that someone, forgotten, had said, on seeing Naples from the water: 'See Naples and die.' Certainly death was not necessary or desirable with so much of the world left still to explore. But in those days Naples was a marvellous experience. I am told that following the wars and bombings of that city, many shattered houses were left largely unrepaired or simply as holes in the ground or piles of rubbish still breathing of wars of destruction. Naples and the country surrounding it, especially to the south, opened a new life for us. The people were glad to see us since visitors in the 1920s were not too frequent.

At that time it was possible to climb Vesuvius. We took a little train which ambled rather whimsically through suburbs and villages filled with the glorious scents of lemons and acacias. The languid calls of the train porters I can still hear: 'Bel-la-Vis-ta' or some other village names. There was a lift up the mountain, but we decided to walk. It was fine at first, but as we neared the top we suddenly realized that our feet were very hot and by the time we reached the observation platform our shoes were wrecks, soles badly burned by contact with hot cinders. We were there long enough to give me a still vivid picture of the inferno of the mountains. A great deal of sulphurous smoke was spurting from the centre core of the mountain's wide mouth, and once or twice there also appeared to be flames. Occasionally we thought we detected rumblings of the earth itself. Our view was interrupted by orders for everyone to leave the mountain immediately. We were hustled into lift cages and lowered quickly down without the usual stopping places. My husband and I then sought a shoe shop for shoes to use for the rest of our holiday. The following day, or perhaps two days later, Versuvius started her 1922 eruption. The city was dark, ominous, sooty and the mountain top disappeared in clouds of soot and ashes. I was anxious to stay and experience the rest of the eruption, but our jobs were forcing us back to England and we had to take the train and leave.

So started my somewhat startling introduction to the beauties and threats of Italy. Also it was my first introduction to what I firmly believed were the habits of all Americans, since almost all on that ship had thrown aside inhibitions, causing one to wonder what life over there could possibly be like. I didn't realize, at that time, that America was in the first throes of Prohibition, and the boat ride offered release.

In the early days of his travels in Europe, Lawrence completed the great walk over the mountains in Switzerland and down into Italy. This story he wrote very vividly and one cannot forget the strange parade of little carved Christos. Later he urged me to repeat the walk, not necessarily following his road, but seeking others for my own story.

Finally such an effort became possible and Lawrence told my husband and me of a good departure point in Switzerland. He also suggested that we should save time and the effort of walking by taking a train through the less interesting parts of the journey to our destination. He warned us, however, that we should not take the 'Rapide', because that was first class and comparatively dull. If we had the time we should take the slower train which included first, second, and third class and which stopped at many stations with constant change of passengers. It would be far more interesting, he said, but we should take our own food.

So we purchased two second-class tickets, joined the train very early to assure ourselves comfortable seats and we were on our way.

For the fullest adventure we should have travelled third class, where there is normally far more action, but the third-class coach was to be dropped from the train sometime before we reached our destination.

We both spoke fairly understandable French. We also had studied and knew adequate Italian, so we felt prepared for passengers moving from France to Italy. We were a little shocked, however, to find that the other passengers in our compartment were German, so that any communication in the beginning was almost impossible.

This was a sad train, as so many people were saying farewell. A mother was seeing her eighteen-year-old son off to a job a long way from home. She was weeping and the son seemed embarrassed. A young couple were in one another's arms, both crying because they must part. So at first there was an air of gloom in the coaches.

The whole train had corridors from end to end so that, with the exception of the first class, which was sealed off, there was intercommunication. Apart from the constant change of passengers at small stations the first part of the journey was uneventful, but always interesting.

When evening approached we were already in the mountains and the changes of light from valley to hill as we climbed were endlessly fascinating. Soon the evening began to advance, rapidly folding the valleys in a violet tinted blueness of approaching night. The high snowcapped peaks became flaming torches where the last rays of sun were trapped to burn briefly.

One by one the compartments emptied. The train became quiet as almost everyone moved to the corridor to get a better view of the splendour of the passing day. The blue of the valleys deepened. The flames of the high peaks burned with renewed and fiercer energy. Suddenly a voice a little way down the corridor started singing softly, a gentle and slightly melancholy song suited to the dying day. After a few lines of music others who knew the song joined in, and softly and rhythmically the train moved on from one day into the unknown tomorrow. The peaked flames died and we were left with the faint outline of greying snow. The blue of the valleys turned almost to black. The song ceased and we all returned to our seats in the compartments.

Somehow those magic moments released a semblance of brotherhood and we all started talking together. The German of our companions was understandable through gesture and laughter. From the depth of our luggage we drew strangely assorted foods which we shared with one another. My husband and I were faced with horrendous-looking and smelling German sausages which we had to share and, for friendship's sake, did not dare refuse. We for our part passed out apples and cheese and black bread. It was wonderful how five to ten minutes of a rare beauty in the past scene changed personalities and opened doors of understanding.

Considerable wine was consumed by our fellow passengers and later we all settled quietly in the cramped space of our individual seats, some of us even sleeping – judging by the loud snores. We had removed our shoes for added comfort and the smells of feet mixed happily with those of garlic sausage and wine.

So passed the night to another day, and possibly another country. Once again Lawrence, who was introducing us to his own world of adventures, had given us a lovely adventure of our own.

Lawrence gave us many verbal directions to other interesting and romantic places to visit, such as Gardone on Lake Garda. From there, on his advice, we took the little steamer trips along with sheep, crates of chickens, calves, and the rugged human passengers, stopping at other little lake villages right up to Riva in the Tyrol. There we discovered a wonderful craft shop where an old man whittled out amazing figures from wood, with movable limbs attached to the main body by strings that one could pull, thus creating a wooden puppet show. Being limited by space and weight I bought a small bear: when I pulled the string the bear danced!

Wherever Lawrence sent us wonders were disclosed. I remember his saying that we must go to Venice because it was another experience. In the case of Venice he even told us where we should stay, this being a little house on the Grand Canal owned and operated as a rooming house by two fussy old ladies. He told us it would all be very simple, which it was, but the old ladies were very kind and excellent cooks, also true statements.

From the window of our living room we looked out on the Grand Canal where the life of Venice existed. The lights over the water at night and the long shadows were endlessly fascinating. At that time there were almost no mechanical boats and certainly no water buses to foul the water, pollute the air, and threaten the foundations of buildings. Travel was mostly by gondola, and at night the strange eerie cries of the gondoliers warned others of their kind at canal corners. We were singularly fortunate because the second day of our visit was the opening of two days of Grand Canal festivities. It was very exciting with all the lights at night, decorated barges and public exuberance. St Mark's Square, always so beautiful, gained a new dimension, a new reality, in the festivities of a generation new to its antiquities.

So it was wherever we went. Inspired by Lawrence everything gained heightened joy. He said little in his directions which in themselves were usually simple, but loaded with the promise of a quality of new interest, even excitement.

Lawrence's gentle kindness was responsible for my meeting many interesting people of the time. At his suggestion I was invited to the house of Koteliansky ('Kot'), a seemingly powerful and rather overwhelming man with heavy arms and legs that appeared not to belong to his slender body. At his house I had my first cup of Russian tea, made in a genuine and rather beautiful samovar. I was given strange little Russian cakes and felt extremely sophisticated. As the visit ended so did the momentarily acquired sophistication, as I realized that Kot had been rather bored by my company.

When Lawrence was told that we were going to Paris, he said: 'So, you are coming to Europe and Paris. I want you to meet Raymond Duncan who lives there.' I was thrilled beyond words at this possibility, since I had seen his sister Isadora dance and, because of my two years of ballet training, I was impressed by her new methods.

Lawrence wrote a little note to Duncan introducing us. He left this letter open for us to read, and it is suggestive of his kindness and tact that instead of indicating that we would like to meet Duncan, he wrote words to this effect: that he was sending friends who I am sure you would like to meet and will find very interesting. We had difficulty in finding Duncan at the address given by Lawrence and wandered rather dismally up and down the street looking for the house number. Soon I spotted a man very queerly dressed who disappeared down a side alley, and to the distress of my husband I ran after him. Almost immediately he too vanished through a rather forlorn-looking door. Reaching the entrance I knocked. The door was mysteriously opened and I was invited in, followed by my extremely worried companion. We entered a large room, the walls of which, to my memory, were hung with lengths of material in the form of drapes. It was a little gloomy inside, but there were a number of people seated on the floor or standing talking. Obviously they knew one another, but they greeted the two strangers who had just joined them. We were invited to be seated on cushions on the floor. There did not appear to be any chairs. I noted that one corner of the room was curtained off. Before long the eyes of those present seemed to be directed towards this curtain. Presently everyone fell silent, the curtains parted and Raymond appeared, an astonishing figure in a Greek-style toga, sandals and beads. His greying hair was very long, down to his shoulders, and he fixed brilliant eyes on us – the new arrivals! I handed him Lawrence's letter and as he read it carefully his eyes fixed steadily on me. My memory tells me that he said: 'You are welcome.' Immediately the session, or whatever it was called, commenced. Raymond Duncan read some poems that were unknown to me. Then he read poems he had composed, these with a metre I had never heard. He read something, either poem or prose, in a foreign language that I found out later was Greek. The session went on and on, I becoming more and more uncomfortable as I realized that those startling eyes were fixed on us, and more particularly on me.

I myself was somewhat strangely attired. I felt at that time my sartorial appearance would be appropriate for Paris. It consisted of a dress woven in peasant style, then called a djibber. The garment itself had a front-laced bodice and a full skirt. The front panel of the bodice and the neck and sleeve openings were embroidered with a design made by my husband and executed by myself. With the djibber I wore a plain white blouse with full sleeves also hand-made. At that time I had made a leather jacket, the parts joined together by leather thongs of the same colours as the embroidery. This was topped by a large black felt hat of somewhat witch-like appearance. Before the arrival at Duncan's lecture room I had felt suitably dressed for sophisticated Paris. But under the close scrutiny of those penetrating eyes, I began to doubt the suitability of my whole attire.

During the reading small cups of Turkish coffee were handed around silently. Little cakes were given and I tasted my coffee. It was my first introduction to the Turkish type and was very strong, seemed thick and rather sweet, so thick that the spoon appeared to stand upright in it! The taste was to me extraordinary and must, I felt, be one acquired, but I pretended to like it, showing myself that pretence can be an early part of education.

Finally the readings came to an end and people began to wriggle and shuffle on the cushioned floor-seats. Only then did Raymond speak. In a soft voice he told us that our visit was welcome and that he would meet us again in a few days, privately, so that we could talk. That second visit, however, never took place. We left Paris before the date arrived, headed for Avignon, the bridge on which one danced, and the Palace of the Popes. I have always regretted being unable to respond to that invitation for the second visit. Somehow that early meeting with Raymond Duncan has remained a permanent and vivid picture in my memory; possibly those staring eyes are responsible.

On another occasion I was taken to some strange house in, I think, the Bloomsbury district of London and there was introduced to Virginia Woolf. She eyed me coldly up and down, and was obviously not the least bit interested in this conventionally dressed country bumpkin from the Midlands. In an icy voice, she said 'How do you do?' and her attention drifted to the strangely assorted groups of her own kind. I was later told that Virginia was known for frequent rudeness and apparent superiority, but, it was explained, these moments occurred for the most part when she was suffering one of her many periods of illness. As with Raymond Duncan's eyes, which at least were accepting and searching, Virginia's coldness has remained fixed in my memory. I knew my inferiority in her group and needed no chill reminder.

My husband and I continued to visit Italy as frequently as possible. On at least two occasions we arrived at some appointed meeting place to find the Lawrences had been obliged to move, due to illness on the part of Bert. Such sudden moves could be from the ocean to the mountains when Lawrence was bothered by one of his 'attacks'. Through the long period of sickness Lawrence always denied the illness, declaring it was the place where he was currently staying that did not agree with him. It made him ill, he said, and then moved. He had no patience with people who used bodily weakness as an excuse. He was very critical of Katherine Mansfield because, he said, she made use of her own diseases. From my one visit to Katherine, I am inclined to believe Lawrence's objections, although my experience causes me to wonder whether the 'show' which she sometimes put on was not really organized by Middleton Murry. On this one visit I noted Katherine to be extremely pale and wearing a long, very dark-coloured full-skirted gown that somehow increased her pallor, lying on a couch with the long dark skirt draped around her. She made a beautiful, almost exquisite picture. Numerous friends were present on that visiting day, and Murry stood at the foot of her couch gazing at her with wide-open, adoring eyes. For some strange reason I was not impressed, sensing a show for the benefit of the company. Such an exhibition would have been abhorrent to Lawrence. Katherine was, however, very beautiful in her pallor and other-worldliness.

Lawrence attached the blame for his physical problems on defective housing which caused a bad cold, or on some other malevolent aspect of the town or surroundings. In this way he didn't allow the tuberculosis which was developing to interfere with his travel. Our first visit to the Villa Mirenda outside Florence was typical. We had been given directions, told to take a tram to the nearby village of Vingone, then walk a certain distance up the highway until we came to a side-road marked by two large cypress trees. We were to follow that road until we reached the villa. There we found Lawrence ill in bed. We could not stay there because, Frieda said, his nights were very disturbed. They had a room for us at a little bar-restaurant in Vingone village. Lawrence explained it was a very nice place to stay because the visitors' windows opened out to a wide balcony where breakfast was served out of doors in the Italian spring sunshine. It was indeed a simple but lovely spot, chosen by Lawrence, and its simplicity and beauty were infinitely preferable to a hotel.

At the Mirenda during the day, Lawrence was propped up in bed with many pillows, knees bent up with a writing pad on the uplifted legs, allowing him to write just as if he were not totally incapacitated. Frieda would be working in the kitchen, struggling to start a fire in the difficult stove so that she could cook the meal. She mumbled and fussed at the stove acquiring smudges of coal dust on her face. At intervals Lawrence called her into the bedroom and read to her what he had just written. Sometimes they laughed together and at other times she would sound a little shocked and in her deep, throaty voice, said: 'Lorenzo, you cannot say that.' Usually he ignored her warnings and did say it. These domestic interludes became very precious to me.

The following story is well known from, I believe, frequent repetition, each story slightly different from the others. Frieda herself gave me this version, her amused green eyes enjoying her own wickedness. She had left Lawrence alone in Italy visiting, if memory serves, the Huxleys in Forte di Marme. She went to visit the exhibition of Lawrence's paintings in London. All went well for a few days, then Lawrence became extremely ill and returned to Florence. Pino Orioli, with whom Lawrence was staying, was very distressed since there seemed to be nothing he could do to help his guest. I believe Frieda told me a doctor was called, but no relief was gained. Pino became frightened since the invalid seemed to be close to death, and decided to call and inform Frieda. This he did and she said she would return immediately. From my memories of the story, Lawrence was told of her pending arrival. Soon Frieda returned from Germany and walked into her husband's sick-room. In the meantime, although it certainly was not peach season in Italy, someone had brought the sick man a bowl of peaches and there it sat upon the table. Entering the room Frieda saw the peaches and taking no notice of Lawrence, cried out: 'Oh, peaches, how wonderful', whereupon she picked one up and started eating. The dying man was furious she had not advanced in his direction. In his bed he pulled himself together, and although he had not walked for days he got out of bed and almost thundered across the room at Frieda, snatching the nibbled peach from her hand, and throwing it at her! The man, sick to the point of death, was almost instantly cured. Frieda told me that she knew exactly how to bring her husband out of one of those attacks if she had been absent at the time. 'You see,' she said, 'he needed me and he needed the rage that I produced in him. It brought back his vitality!'

When we visited the Mirenda, Lawrence told us of the interesting cafés to visit in Florence. As we sat and drank our morning coffee we were told where to buy fascinating and delicious little Florentine cookies. He mentioned galleries and museums not regularly visited, but holding spectacular exhibits. 'Go to Fiesole just before sunset', he said, urging us to go up the hills behind the town and then watch the sun set over Florence and the lights begin to sparkle in the city, the last rays of light catching the spires of the town's buildings like torches in the sky. He said, too, that if we could find a place to stay it would be delightful to get up before dawn and watch morning taking the city in the arms of the coming day.

William and Sallie Hopkin early in their marriage, before the turn of the century

William and Sallie Hopkin, photographed during days of long walks

Enid Hopkin – aged about sixteen months. The embroidered dress was made by Sallie Hopkin

Enid Hopkin – 'that haughty Enid' – aged about four, outside her home in Eastwood

Enid Hopkin aged three

Runswick Bay, Whitby, Yorkshire, in the early 1900s. Enid, aged seven, is seated between her parents, nursing the family cat

Enid Hopkin on the coast of Scotland, aged about eleven.

Enid Hopkin reading poetry to friends, c. 1910

The first tram in Eastwood, 1913

Eastwood: a procession of striking miners, 1911

D.H. Lawrence in his pram

D.H. Lawrence on his twenty-first birthday, 1906

Villa Mirenda: a card sent by D.H. Lawrence to his sister Emily, February 1927

Lawrence and Frieda at the Villa Mirenda, c. 1927

Enid Hilton in her late fifties

Photographs on pages 5, 6 and 7 of the plate section are reproduced by kind permission of Keith Sagar

Lawrence told us stories of vendettas between houses still being carried on in the nearby Tuscany hills. We found these a little amusing because the participants were extremely careful that domestic hatreds did not result in any deaths. They loved the romance and made much to-do about the vendettas, but were amusingly cautious over preservation of their own lives. 'It was a sort of a game with them,' he said. 'You must come at Easter time and see the processions winding through the vineyards and up the paths of the scrubby hillsides. It is really very beautiful with candles and lamps of the softly-singing groups climbing the winding paths through the bush and led by a statue of the Virgin leaning a little tipsily sometimes by worshippers who were themselves a little tipsy, but not from the angle of the climb as in the case of the Virgin.'

On another occasion when we visited the Lawrences I was asked if I could type decently enough for my work to be legible. I replied that I could, but I had never been taught the skill, simply because typing lessons were not given in school in my time. Having decided that the ability to type was a necessity for me, I taught myself. Self-imposed lessons had resulted in a 'hunt and peck' ability, fairly fast and usually legible. Lawrence seemed satisfied and asked if I'd care to type a small book for him, the story being in manuscript. He explained the demand on my time by the fact that the book was quite unusual and that if a local Italian typist knew enough to translate it, she would also know too much and be very shocked, with who knew what results! He had asked me, he said, because he knew that even if shocked, I would remain uncritical, yet interested and free of judgement. So I left Italy with the manuscript of a book then titled *The Escaped Cock*. I had been asked to make three copies, then return all three to Lawrence. This I did, finding the story very intriguing, though a little beyond my understanding. The title of the story was later changed since Lawrence himself felt that the cockerel title was a little suggestive to the uninitiated. The new title given was *The Man Who Died*. Apparently my hunt and peck typing from the manuscript proved satisfactory, since the book was published under its new title.

On one visit to the Mirenda when Lawrence was not sick, he told us of another book he had just finished writing. He told us that it had been published in Italy, because it would never be allowed, and because he could not find a publisher in England. It was not a wicked book, he said, but a little advanced for its time and English people were not ready for it. He stated, however, that he badly wanted the book to be introduced in England: and would we be willing to take a few copies back with us, to keep at our apartment until he wrote telling us where and to whom they should be delivered? It is significant in view of Lawrence's puritanism that he asked me in the first instance to be the smuggler, but when I immediately accepted the idea, added that I must not accept until I had discussed it with my husband. 'Never do anything behind his back or without discussion of the idea. Get his approval. Otherwise you may spoil your marriage.' It was discussed with my husband who agreed to be involved. We had not read the book nor did we read it until it was safely in England, so we had no knowledge of its contents. Our agreement was based solely on friendship and in my own case on an infinite and proven faith in the author. There is not much spare room in a knapsack, but my husband took three or four copies hidden at the bottom of his sack. I managed to squeeze a few copies into my own sack and I took a paper bag with three or four copies to carry by hand. We covered them with book jackets displaying innocent titles and pictures and left for England. At points of custom examinations out of Italy and then into England we were not bothered.

Obviously one cannot pack too many sins in a rucksack, which, when glanced into, disclosed clean underwear, an extra pair of shoes, a clean shirt and toiletries. As for my copies in the paper bag, I took them out, folded the bag for future use and hid the copies on my person. In that time athletic women, or those who walked a great deal, wore knickers made of the same material as their dress. These had white cotton detachable linings for laundry purposes and the legs were elasticized. Nearing the place of custom examination I slipped two copies of the book into each knicker leg. This made walking a little difficult and one had to be careful, but the plan worked beautifully. The books arrived at our flat in England and were stashed for safe keeping under my bed.

Soon I received notes asking me to deliver, not send by mail, copies to people whose names were listed. Some of these were out of London, so that I had to take a bus or a train in order to deliver my morally suspicious burden to its new owner. The book, of course, was *Lady Chatterley's Lover*, an innocent enough production in modern times but viewed with horror by British authorities of the day. It was threatened to be withdrawn from further publication and burned, but there were enough less stodgily minded people with sufficient authority to prevent this. I remember with considerable interest that when first I came to America in 1932 I did not find a single person who had read any Lawrence book other than *Lady Chatterley's Lover*. Even then it was read secretly, kept in dark corners of a house or store, to be giggled over by unenlightened friends.

In the meantime my husband and I had bought one of Lawrence's paintings, called 'Fire Dance', depicting a couple dancing in firelight in a forest, really a very charming painting. On one visit to the Lawrences' we were asked if we would take some other paintings that Lawrence had made. He told us very simply that he thought they were good and that a gallery in London had promised to exhibit them, but, he said, they would shock the Victorian-minded British and he could not send them by public carrier. The paintings were removed from their frames for lightness of carriage and covered with copies of famous but more discreet works of art, such as a young and innocent English couple would collect. The paintings were placed in a suitcase, so this time in addition to our rucksacks we carried one item of regular luggage. The suitcase also passed the eagle eyes of the custom inspectors, arrived safely in England, and was stored with the books under my bed until Dorothy Trotter, who owned the gallery, was ready to put them on exhibition. As is now public knowledge, the exhibited paintings caused much comment and some consternation in London.

One day when I visited the gallery Mrs Trotter told me that she had heard through the underground that police had been ordered to raid the gallery and seize the paintings. Mrs Trotter asked me if I would mind delivering a letter to her lawyer. She did not dare to telephone, lest some listening device had been attached to her phone. I left the gallery, and shortly afterwards the police arrived, seizing thirteen pictures, and arresting everyone in the gallery. I avoided that indignity merely by not being there at the moment of police activity. The story of the pictures and the fight to avoid their being burned is well known.

Naturally these were exciting times. One felt part of an enormous conspiracy to broaden the stodgy views of an island which was still Victorian in its attitudes. It was all part of the larger world, and heightened adventures of the Lawrences during those days.

After the episodes of books and paintings we saw little of the Lawrences in either England or abroad. Lawrence's condition was worsening steadily and while I joined him in denial of his illness, yet I was forced to accept his developing silence and lack of contact.

The news of Lawrence's death in 1930 was a terrible shock to me. I felt as if half my life had passed away with him, as was almost the case. Somehow I had felt that he would be eternal, as indeed in another sense he has proved to be. We were unable to attend the funeral in Vence, France, due to our respective jobs, but as soon as we could arrange a vacation we went to Vence and to Frieda, who was still living there. Unfortunately we could not stay in the house since there were other guests already installed. Frieda found lodgings for us in a charming nearby cottage. I remember that cottage so well, its surroundings soothing my grief. The bedroom was long and low with a similarly shaped window surrounded by a lemon-tree in blossom. The perfume of the lemon was almost overpowering, seeming to permeate the whole world, since it accompanied one long after departure from it. At night a nightingale sat either in the lemon tree or in an adjoining bush and sang his heart out. In a small pond, part of the cottage garden, was a frog who, even at the wrong time of year, croaked his contribution to the chorus. Yes, indeed, Frieda had chosen a soul-soothing spot.

The day after our arrival we were asked if we wanted to go to the cemetery and see the grave. Since others were going we joined them and set off on a bright morning. I remember so well that Pino Orioli was one of the group. Pino was a funny little man, funny in the sense of amusing, and quick at repartee, loaded with humorous remarks. His presence was helpful on such a saddening journey. I remember standing in a shocked group, eyes fixed on the grave, which was headed by a picture in rocks showing Lawrence's symbolic phoenix. I only dimly realized at that time that the headstone was a prediction. Lawrence had indeed risen from the ashes of his grave to heights then undreamed.

The sad group left the cemetery in silence, all of us trying not to cry. Such tears would be disliked by the dead man. Pino came to the rescue in his usual humorous way. He told us we should stop at a cafe, sit quietly for a while and drink some coffee. This we did and at the cafe, Pino disappeared with the waiter. When the two reappeared, the waiter was carrying the coffee. Pino was carrying tiny glasses of some liqueur. He handed one of these to each of us and told us to drink it along with the coffee and we would feel better. Unsuspectingly we thought perhaps it was a good idea. We had already begun the coffee, and seemed to wait a short time before trying the liqueur. I think Frieda was the first taster, and she pronounced it pleasant. After a few minutes she looked around the table and to our horror started laughing. In the meantime other people had sipped and, as with Frieda, in a few minutes they too began to laugh. The rest of us who had been more abstemious were horrified. What was the matter with these grieving people? Was the group becoming subject to grief-propelled hysteria? And if so, what had produced it? My husband and I had not yet sampled our drinks. Then he attacked his tiny glass and to my amazement, since he was normally a very quiet man, he sputtered into his glass and found the whole situation hilarious. To drown my annoyance with him I sipped on my own glass and within a very few minutes I thought the scene was a scream and laughed accordingly. Soon we were all transformed from misery-racked individuals to a happy laughing small crowd unable to control their mirth. Then I noticed that Pino himself was the only one without a glass. I asked him laughingly why he hadn't joined us and he replied it was better for him to remain without the stimulating joy so that he could pay the bill and make necessary explanations. Certainly these were in order and when our laughter had subsided a little he told us that he had felt the urge to dispel the gloom, so he had suggested the coffee and followed that up with his own idea of breaking the misery with what he called the 'Laughing Liqueur'. In his Italian way he was certainly successful.

Frieda indicated that she was returning to England and would appreciate my help with the problems that emerged from the fact that Lawrence died intestate. Frieda felt that since she was his wife and had nursed him, enduring his illness-induced irritations and changeability, and stimulating his writing, she was entitled to custody of the literary estate and any funds that the couple had possessed. The family, on the other hand, believed that everything belonged to them. With the exception of Ada, Lawrence's youngest sister, the rest of the family had never really accepted Frieda. On her return to England the fight was at its height, and even Ada told Frieda, either by word of mouth or by letter, that she hated her from the bottom of her heart. Frieda herself told me this, looking at me with strange, almost unseeing eyes, and remarked: 'I think it must be terrible to hate anyone from the bottom of the heart. I don't think I could do that.'

In the meantime the question of disposal of the estate had become a matter of court order. It was decided by the court, as far as my memory serves, that money from the estate should go to Frieda, since she was so deeply involved in his books. Any money in any bank account went to the family. Since the ultimate value of the estate could not then be determined it seemed that Frieda had an unknown share, but she was happy. I'm not sure of the correctness of my information, but I know that Frieda's children were involved.

At the time of Frieda's return to England I was not working, so I could spend much of my time with her in a Temperance Hotel.

She almost apologized for her choice of residence, but remarked that although the other occupants were dull and stuffy for the most part there were not wild parties, and she could sleep. Everything about her room was higgledy-piggledy and out of order, with Frieda frequently leaving important legal papers in a chaos of underwear, ribbons, and private letters. She mentioned sadly that she would need me to help her sort out the mess and put things in order. She told me that one of the first things Lawrence had taught her in the early days was how to arrange her affairs. He had shown her that she must put her stockings in one place, underwear in another, with neatly piled blouses somewhere else. Papers must be separated, important ones here, letters in another place, and so forth, but after his death somehow this order had been abandoned.

There were many difficulties associated with the rearranging of things, but somehow after a few days Frieda's chaos was reduced to some sort of order. One worthwhile story is associated with the disorder. At one point I discovered in a pile of old papers an almost frightening souvenir of their early days together. This was a toy model of a spider, quite a big one and cleverly made to be alarming if seen at the wrong moment. The creature itself had a fur-covered body to give some semblance of reality, and black legs made out of fine springs, so that they moved almost of their own accord when the thing was touched. Glaring black and white eyes painted on the head added to the scariness. Frieda told me the story of the spider.

One day she and Lawrence were looking with interest in the window of a toy shop. Frieda, who had her own childish moments, fell in love with the creature and asked Lawrence if she could buy it. It was only a few pennies. Lawrence was horrified at the idea of wasting their dwindled resources on such a foolish purchase. Frieda said that she argued with him. It was so long since she had had any money or any fun for herself. Everything was always poverty, poverty. Yet Lawrence remained firm in his refusal. She was sad. She said the picture of the spider haunted her and the next day she stole the required pennies from their household account, returned to the store and bought the monstrosity. For several weeks Frieda enjoyed its companionship. Then Lawrence discovered it. They had one of their first real hurting quarrels, but she hung on to the spider.

'Now,' she said, 'I don't really like it any more and I want you to take it, so that I know it is still around, but I do not want hurting incidents to be part of my memory or to recur to me any time I look at the spider. I want my memories of Lawrence at that time to be clear of unhappiness.'

I still have the spider in my possession, a battered, mangled specimen with bent, lifeless legs, very little fur on the body and, I think, one glaring eye left. So much for the battered remains of our unhappiness.

After the settlement of the estate Frieda returned to the Lawrence Ranch, approximately twenty miles into the mountains beyond Taos, New Mexico. I had a sad feeling that my Lawrence days were over, but this dismal thought, however, turned out to be untrue.

Soon after Lawrence's death Frieda and Aldous Huxley together decided that many of Lawrence's letters addressed to friends or critics in many parts of the world should be preserved, since they were of interest not only to the original recipients. Such letters, however, could be angry to the point of literary violence and were unsuitable for immediate publication. The final plan was for the volume to be compiled by Aldous Huxley after careful selection of the material to be included. The next question was who would type copies of the letters and be responsible for their return to their rightful owners? Several people were suggested, but Frieda felt that many of those opened doors to almost worldwide gossip. Finally my name was suggested. This selection was not exactly flattering. Obviously I knew few of the interesting owners of the more scandalous letters, so I could not be guilty of gossip. I was approached and accepted the commission. The final plan was for Aldous to write to the more famous recipients of the correspondence, and Lawrence's letters were to be forwarded to Aldous by registered mail. Certain of the letters I myself requested, and in this way another close connection with Lawrence was established. It was quite hard, responsible work but intensely interesting. After copies were completed all were returned by registered mail to their rightful owners. Occasionally, as his employment permitted, my husband would help with a little of the typing. As this was completed I sorted the letters into three separate piles arranged according to my judgement; whether they were immediately publishable, were unsuitable for publication for some years, and those that I could not judge. At intervals Aldous Huxley visited my apartment, collecting finished letters for return to their owners and checking my suggestions of now or later or undecided. Generally Aldous approved of my selections.

Those were indeed quite wonderful days. I became more closely knowledgeable of Lawrence's connections with a world wider than I had ever suspected. Also I knew far more about Aldous Huxley and became aware of his brilliant and sensitive mind.

My husband and I had started a small collection of French and Italian hand-crafted pottery of which several examples were scattered about our apartment. We were at that time sharing a house at 44 Mecklenberg Square with R.H. Tawney, an historian, in Bloomsbury, and we had a large first-floor room with space for the exhibits. I remember Aldous talking about the letters, walking up and down the room, picking up here one piece of pottery, there another, nodding his approval if he liked that specimen, or returning it silently to its shelf if he had no use for it.

After work on the letters had been completed Frieda wanted to pay me, but I felt that payment had been already made through the enlargement of my life and the vast experience to which I had been exposed through the letters themselves. Subsequently Frieda sent me a second-class boat ticket to America so I could visit the Lawrence ranch in New Mexico. She remarked simply that Lawrence would have liked that. I exchanged the second-class billet, and added a little money for two tourist-class tickets so my husband could accompany me. Thus Lawrence once again was exposing me to new living conditions and people, broadening my horizons even into a new world. Once more my days were given a magical quality through my Lawrence connection. And D.H. Lawrence continues to be so much with me. In my old age I look back and see a kind, fun-loving man, sensitive to the extreme, and uncannily knowledgeable of the dreams and perhaps fears of a child. His death seemed to be the end of everything, yet he has continued to be part of my life, so much so that I feel it to be almost a duty and certainly a necessity to show to the world my experiences of and with a subtly complex man.

Rainbows and Pots of Gold

To my son Colin for his infinite patience, his encouragement, and his perseverance.

Foreword

———

Enid Hilton came to Mendocino County in the 1940s. The stories which follow are some of the many experiences she encountered along Mendocino County's distant hills and backroads during the 1940s and 1950s. As a transplanted Englishwoman she found tales of magnificent courage, love and dedication in these regions, before they were lost to the chaos of progress. She wrote these pieces to share the experiences, dreams and insights of her ninety-six years, finishing the work shortly before she died.

MARGARET WILLIAMSON

Acknowledgements

Thanks to my father for introducing me to the wild world and expressing to me its poetry.

My thanks also to Dr Annette White-Parks for her help in taking dictation and transcribing the material for this book. And also thanks and appreciation to Mary Exworthy and Margaret Williamson for their help in typing the stories.

And last but not least to the people of the stories for their endless courage and enduring adaptations to difficult circumstances.

Introduction

The following stories are all true. They are simple because the people written about lived a less complicated life than one finds in the 1990s. They tell of another period in history – one which will never return. They are stories of courage, of making the most of what you have, and sometimes of a final achievement. Indeed they are small histories of the formation of Western America by people who never recognized defeat.

Names and places have been changed, locations sometimes shuffled around to preserve confidentiality and privacy. Some of the stories emphasize road conditions and describe difficulties encountered in reaching remote homes. This problem of access is a necessary part of the history. Freeways were only a dream of the future – a type of transportation science fiction. Today, however, the dream highway is a reality and freeways take us into and out of the wild country.

Rarely today, if ever, does one find a lonely cabin out in the wilderness occupied by some abandoned old man drowning his sorrows in intoxication. The cabins have gone and the wild hills are now open to off-road vehicles that fill the formerly cool, damp recesses of the forest with petrol fumes.

Life moves on. It must. But in that movement so much of beauty and struggle is lost that the gains rarely compensate.

These stories are written in the hope that their resurrection will remind us of simpler days when 'doing without' or 'making do with' produced a strong and vibrant society capable of entering a very different phase of human life and making a success of the new and mechanized world in which we now live.

CHAPTER ONE

Appointments

The letter was on my desk on Monday morning. It was written in round, boyish handwriting, meticulously composed on ruled writing pad paper. It asked the kind consideration of the Department in sending a worker to interview a Mr Carl Hansen, and prepare to assist him in an application for medical and other benefits. He was crippled, unable to drive, and no longer employable. To this date friends had been supporting him, but could no longer afford the necessary medical care. He would, of course, be very grateful for any assistance given to him. There followed instructions for reaching his home, which he said he shared with two other friends, and the letter ended.

I knew it would be a long drive, since the home was on a side-road between the main highway and the ocean. But the country was beautiful, so the more than sixty miles offered no fears. These narrow, twisty, hilly roads giving access to the coast villages were always interesting, if only for the changing growth of trees and plants as one approached the ocean. Near the highway vegetation was that of the forest, but as one approached the tops of the hills and the downgrade towards the sea there were visible and rapid changes of scenery, always fascinating.

I contacted Mr Hansen giving a date and a possible time of arrival and, according to plan, started early on my long journey. The side-road was approximately thirty miles long and soon I arrived at a very small collection of houses, scarcely large enough to be called a village yet sufficient to include the inevitable bar and the small Baptist chapel. Ahead of me I noticed, on the right-hand side of the road, an enormous redwood tree that at some early date had been gutted by fire. The core of the tree had been burned out, but the outer shell survived and continued the tree's growth. In this shell there were quite wide cracks. The largest of these had been shaped into a doorway and a proper door had been installed. The whole tree was a little back from the road, so there was ample space in front for parking and also room for a number of redwood rounds, trimmed and stacked for sale to would-be gardeners.

In front of the open door stood two men. One, about seventy-five, was stocky, solid, and looked practical. The other, considerably younger, was very slender, blonde, and moved awkwardly. The thin man disclosed that he was Mr Hansen. The other was introduced as Mr Roberts. Their friend, the third one of the trio, was employed part-time at the mill. He was Mr McAlister, old enough to retire but given light part-time work because he preferred to be employed. He would return in about fifteen minutes, I was told.

We entered the tree through the manufactured door, and I was amazed to find quite a lot of space, adequate for a small sitting room in the tree's interior. There were a round table, three stools and a chair with a broken back for visitors. There were also lights in the room. Then I noticed that three other wide cracks in the tree's interior doors led to extensions of the home. One door, partly opened, showed a neat and tidy lean-to building used as a bedroom. It was all immaculate with three cots, clean bedding, beds made, sheets turned down over smooth blankets. Each bed had a box at its foot and pegs were driven into the bark of the tree to hold Sunday clothes. Another door, wide open, revealed a small kitchen, with shelves for china and cutlery resting upside down on jars, and all the usual needs of a cook. It was all so ingenious, so beautifully planned and arranged that it appeared almost commodious.

I turned my sightseeing to business and explained to Mr Hansen what he would have to do to apply for medical assistance, on the one hand, and a supporting grant on the other. As usual it was all unnecessarily complicated, but we got everything filled out in a manner that would be satisfactory for the county's needs and information. When I was taking particulars from Mr Hansen he showed me his hands, which were severely crippled by arthritis, the fingers bent back into hook-like claws, and virtually useless.

'You see,' said Mr Hansen, 'I can no longer use my hands and sometimes they are extremely painful. My feet are the same way. If you wish, I will show you my feet. They are very clean.'

I assured Mr Hansen that foot inspection was not necessary at this point.

A sturdy figure appeared in the door to the street, and Mr McAlister returned from work. A sturdy, efficient Scotsman, he introduced himself and the four of us settled down for more general talk. The three men, so different in type and manner, each contributed much history and observation to the session.

Mr Hansen, disappearing at one point, returned with a very substantial cake and a steaming pot of coffee. A piece of cake was cut for each of us and coffee poured into mugs. I must say that the coffee, very strong, smelled better than it tasted. The cake, a fruit variety, was something else. I quickly discovered that it was a little gritty and assumed that when its baker had learned to cook, the fact it was wise to wash his raisins before including them in the batter had not been part of the lesson. The cake itself had a sharp, unusual flavour. Mr Hansen apologized, explaining that he found, too late, that there was no shortening in the house. So he purified bacon grease and substituted that. After the first few bites it was not at all bad, but to begin with it was a bit of a shock.

As we talked, Mr McAlister told us that the mill had been owned by one family for many generations. As far as was possible it was operated by the owners on a father to son basis – the workmen being engaged in the same plan. 'We are really like one big family,' said Mr McAlister. 'In fact, one of the workmen lost his life defending the mill from the fire because he wondered what his son, then sixteen, would do for employment on graduation from high school if the mill burned.'

Mr Roberts was the practical man of the three friends. He had built the additional sheds that surrounded the tree, made a passable kitchen from one and a usable bedroom from another. He also pointed out with great pride that they had a bathroom with hot water and a primitive shower, the latter consisting of an elaborate system of ropes and pulleys that were held high above the heads of the bathers and distributed hot water through holes in a large metal pail. The only disadvantage, perhaps, lay in the fact that one had to bathe quickly so that the amount of water was adequate for complete cleanliness. Mr Roberts confessed that, before compulsory retirement he'd been a carpenter and a plumber and he liked continuing his trade when and where it was possible. Mr Hansen did as much of the cooking as he could. He gathered the wild berries for pies and made watercress salads from a bed that was in a large pond behind the house. His activities were limited by the hooked hands and, presumably, feet, but he was able to contribute to the general support.

Mr Roberts and Mr Hansen had wonderful stories of flowers and berries that belonged to both types of plant growth – that of the forest and of the nearby ocean. I was told that next year I must come to see them early in the season when wild strawberries and raspberries were ripe; but I must promise not to tell anyone about the raspberries, because Mr Hansen appeared to be the only one who knew about the bed, and there were just enough each year to make one jar of prized jam and one pie. Thimble berries were plentiful a little nearer to the coast and later on, naturally, many beautiful blackberries. So their fruit intake was solved by the invalid, Mr Hansen. Each man had a definite skill, and by joining together in one habitation they were free to exercise those skills – apparently as long as physical ability would allow.

There was another round of cake and coffee. Time was passing and I knew I must leave – leave this dream house, this fairy house, these magical men. One could dream oneself into a philosophy based on grit and bacon-greased cake. These three men had within themselves the quality that had helped make America, giving it the sturdy foundation of mixed cultural levels and abilities. Even my dream was part of the foundation of America – everything starts with a dream, even an adventure.

Sadly I collected my papers, helped by the men, and left through Mr Roberts' front door. I started the car anticipating another kind of magic, the turbulent ocean and its shore growth of seaside villages. I glanced in the rear-view mirror and noted the three men standing outside the door waving goodbye. I honked the horn to acknowledge them, then turned the corner past the bar and the Baptist chapel on the road to my next appointment.

CHAPTER TWO

The Veil

The road to the Masons' house was little more than grass-grown land climbing steeply up the hillside, at first parallel to the main road. The local Highway Patrol man warned me that the lane was not kept up and that I should stay on the inside as far as possible, since the outside edges were subject to crumbling and could let one down on to the heads of travellers on the highway below. Heeding his warning I successfully completed the first part of the treacherous trail, to a point where the road turned sharply left and steeply up a forested hillside. After approximately a half-mile of climbing the track suddenly flattened and widened, revealing a flat area with a small house on the left and enough room in front of it for cars to turn. I noticed a small, deer-fenced garden sloping gently on the right and filled with vegetables. There were struggling flowers around the cottage and it was all very neat and orderly.

A tall, thin man seated on a bench beside the door rose as the car approached, indicating where it was best to park. He was very polite, helped me out of the car and started to lead me towards the door. Suddenly he stopped and in a low voice asked me not to express shock or surprise when I saw his wife. He explained that she had developed some skin disease that, to date, the doctors had been unable to diagnose or cure. This was centred around her mouth and chin, and was unpleasant to see since it consisted of dripping sores. To my inquiry, he said no, they did not at the present time consider it cancerous.

'But you never know . . .' and his voice trailed off. 'You will see how my wife has coped with the situation. Please make no remarks.'

We entered the house directly into the living room, and I noted a slender woman who must at one time have been pretty and was still blessed with quite beautiful dark eyes, expressive and a little sad. Below her nose and round her face fastened to the back of her head was a soft, silky, pale pink veil, hanging down loosely to her chest rather in the manner of a yashmak. With her husband's help she answered all the questions that were asked, but gave no extended information. Her speech was slow and a little restricted, as if talking was painful. She never mentioned her conditions. Certainly her whole appearance was a shock. The strange impression of the veil, however, was offset by the normality of everything else around her. It was an ordinary little room, the furniture adequate, simple and homelike. Part of the walls were papered with a modest pattern. The remaining wall space was painted in soft tones. The commonplace appearance of the room, though, was altered by an unusual lantern with Oriental overtones hanging in the window. In some way the lantern added a new significance to the room.

When the necessary papers were signed I realized that it would be kind to avoid continuing the interview. We talked a little on general affairs. Mrs Mason offered coffee and cookies to see me on the long return journey. I remarked on the lantern, asking its history.

'That was a gift from Korea,' she said, 'during that war.' She offered no explanation of the donor of the gift, then said: 'I think it is very pretty and I light it every night.'

I mentioned their prosperous looking garden then, gently shaking hands and, promising to return shortly, I left the house. Outside and beside my car, Mr Mason and I talked. He told me that he had difficulties with neighbours who were pressuring him into placing his wife in a rest home where she might be adequately cared for medically. But he said he would never do that, 'You do not abandon a woman of courage because her face has become unsightly.'

Then he told me of the later days of the Depression – when they were very poor, he had no job, no Government help was forthcoming, and it was difficult to stay alive.

'This woman never grumbled or complained, but made soups out of weeds, grass, and anything I was able to bring home after a trip with my gun.' He said that he remembered his wife crying as she plucked some bluejay he had shot, or a rabbit, or even a squirrel – local birds or beasts that had become our friends – to add nourishment to her soup. This grim period lasted many weeks, but she never faltered or failed.

I had noticed in the application a mention of two sons. I inquired about them. The man turned away, hiding his face, and told me that at the end of the Vietnam War they had received a notice that their oldest son had been killed in action. This tragic news was followed almost immediately by a further notice that the younger son was reported missing.

The man turned to me: 'It was a dreadful, useless war. A wrong war. And they were very young, not even twenty years old yet.'

Since that time the parents had been seeking the lost boy, through all means of exploring lists of recovered missing persons.

His name never appeared. They heard of other bodies found in the war zones and shipped home, but never that of their son.

'My wife still believes that one day he will be found and returned. My own hope is less strong. Every night she lights the lantern in the window, in case he comes during the dark hours and so that he will know that he is watched for and expected. 'So you see', he said, 'we share a deep grief. Even for me hope is a little restored every night as my wife lights the lamp. We are old, and we will see it through together.'

Mr Mason offered to turn my car for me, since turning space was limited and tricky. This he did, and I made my way down the road to the highway, wondering. Was there some strange connection between the veil hiding one kind of ugliness and grief, and the lantern expressing an eternal hope? There were questions, but few answers.

CHAPTER THREE

The Blind Gardener

Mrs Carpenter, aged ninety-eight, lived in a strange little redwood shack with her much younger husband. Mr Carpenter found life easy with an occasional job and domestic support from his wife's pension. The little house, although primitive in appearance, was very neat and orderly both within and without. There was a substantial vegetable garden and many flowers immediately around the building.

One day, as I was passing the home, I noticed Mrs Carpenter outside working in her flower beds. Her appearance was a little strange because she was wearing a pair of her husband's old shoes far too large for her, and her dress was rolled up around her waist, revealing a dark coloured petticoat and under that one of pink flannel. As always I stopped to greet her, and asked why she was doing that heavy work with a large spade – replanting some chrysanthemums, expected to flower in the autumn.

My concern for Mrs Carpenter was not based merely on her age and the arduous work she was attempting, but I knew that the lady was completely blind. I asked if she could find someone who would do the work for her, since with her condition there were infinite possibilities of injury. Mrs Carpenter snorted, assuring me that already someone had done the work, but, she said, had done it all wrong. I was told that chrysanthemums can be quite fussy about the soil in which they are planted, the correct amount of sunlight and shade, and her assistant had given no thought to any of these important points. 'It was necessary', she said, 'to replant them in places where their wishes would be fulfilled.'

I was puzzled. How did a blind woman know where the plants had been placed? And how could she tell they were not happy with their present home?

I delicately approached these questions which posed no problem for the blind gardener. Mrs Carpenter then told me that she knew everything by *feeling*, and added that she knew by their feel that the chrysanthemums were not happy, and she also knew instinctively that the spots in the garden that she had selected as suitable would be better for the plants, which were her pride and joy in the autumn months.

'If you can't see,' she said, 'you must go by your feelings, and sometimes feeling is better than just seeing, because seeing is only on the surface, but what you feel goes down deep into you.' Even though I had vision, I knew that this blind woman knew more than I would ever know, and I was aware that she did not need my help in her unsighted world. So I left her with her large old shoes and her many petticoats not to mention her heavy shovel, perhaps having gained a little knowledge of myself.

CHAPTER FOUR

A Dark and Stormy Night

It had been a very wet winter. A great deal of rain had already fallen in the area. The land was sodden and the rivers were high. It was a hard time for the poor people, especially those with no transportation. My work was difficult due to slides which frequently blocked the roads or the rivers. When the rivers were blocked the water would then be so high that it undermined the road edges and one could be in danger of going off the road. It was, however, a time when the attention of the welfare worker was most urgently needed. Few of the poorer people had cars that could be trusted to make a journey over rough and deteriorating roads.

On this particular day I had left early on my visiting rounds knowing that there would be difficulties ahead. Quite soon after I left town it started to rain. It was not heavy enough to be threatening, so I continued on my journey. Back in the mountains where many of the poorer people lived the storm gathered strength and the rain poured like a sheet of water descending from heaven to earth.

By this time I was up on the reservation, trying to see that my older clients were protected as far as possible from the onslaught of the winter weather. While there I was given a gift of a large steelhead fish that had been caught by one of the men of the little town. It was quite a heavy fish but I placed it on the back seat of the car where it reposed peacefully. My clients told me that I must leave the small town early, otherwise I would never get home. After all, they said, I could never know whether the road used in the morning would still be there by night in all the rain.

Having finished my work I prepared to leave, putting petrol in the car in case of emergencies. The garage attendant told me that Mrs Johnson, an old blind woman, had no wood for her stove. I turned the car around to investigate. At her one-room cabin I found the information was correct, and she was huddled up trying to keep warm. The man who had promised to deliver wood for her stove had failed to do so. I could not leave her in this condition and started on a round of all the firewood sellers that I knew in the valley. Eventually I found one who was not only willing, but anxious, to supply the missing firewood, along with some dry kindling to be sure that the wet wood could be trusted to burn. Only then did it seem safe to start on the long journey home.

It was already dark and the storm showed no signs of lessening. I hurried over the mountains where the rain was turning into sleet with occasional puffs of snow. Driving fast was impossible, and when I reached the river the usually indolent stream was roaring. So far the bridges I had crossed had held up, but there were others to follow. I also remembered that my flashlight was almost on the point of extinction. My intentions to renew the batteries had not been carried out.

Driving alongside the river was a strange experience. The rain was falling in torrents and the river was roaring to the right of the car. There were many rocks on the road, so travel was slow.

Then in the headlights I saw a mountain of rocks fallen from the high bank to the middle of the road. In winter I always carried in my car a Swedish saw, a shovel, and a mattock-pick. Many times I had found the latter implement very useful in moving heavy rocks from the road, by using the leverage side to raise them and start them rolling, giving enough space for the car to pass.

It was natural for me to stop the car, leaving the engine running, and get out to survey the possibilities of making a passage for myself. Unfortunately this was a big slide, and while I was deciding on the possibility of making a way for the car a fairly large rock came tumbling down and landed on the left side of my head, momentarily knocking me out.

After that bump on the head I think I was not quite sane. What appeared to me to be something of major importance was the care of the fish – the fish and my state papers. What to do now? In this bemused condition I realized that I was only about a mile from a small hamlet where there was a store and friendly store-keepers. In the meantime, another slide behind the car blocked the possibility of return. There appeared to be two choices: either sit in the car and hope that the rest of the mountain wouldn't come tumbling down on me, burying me and the vehicle; or getting out and walking in the rain to the village. I wrapped a blanket over my shoulders and around myself. Realizing in my muddled mind the great importance of the state papers and the fish, I took both of these items with me. I extinguished the lights in the car and locked it (although no one could approach it from either direction) and started stumbling along the road over the fallen rocks to the rear, having bets with myself about how long the flashlight would last.

That was one of the strangest journeys I have ever taken. Naturally the wool blanket was immediately soaked and I tried to seek shelter from riverside bushes where there was actually no shelter – only an acute danger of sliding down into the swollen river. The rain continued to pelt down. It was very dark and the roadway, deep in mud, had many rocks to be negotiated. Obviously it would have been wiser to abandon the blanket, and certainly the fish was not of paramount importance, but my rock-hit head could not fathom such details.

I struggled along to the first bridge, my fading flashlight being of little help. There I noticed a part of the roadway had collapsed, so the remaining entrance to the bridge had to be negotiated with great care. The fish and I manoeuvred our way to the far side. Then, as I turned on to a side-road leading to the village, the flashlight died an untimely death.

The fish, the state papers, and I continued on our way to the second bridge which miraculously was still there. From this point on the road was quite narrow and even more perilous under foot, but there were no rock slides and I was able to reach the village safely.

I made my way up the steps to the front door of the closed store and knocked loudly. There was no sound from within and no sound from the village, except the hammer of the continually pouring rain. I completely failed to rouse the owners of the store. There was no porch or shelter in front of the building, but I remembered that steps along the side walls led up to a small covered rear porch used as a store room. Usually this was kept locked, but fish, blanket, papers, and I clambered up there and found that the screen around the door was partially broken. All I had to do was cover my hand with something to avoid skin tears from loose wires and reach through, releasing the lock from the inside. This accomplished, I was under cover and partially dry although the roof was leaking.

I found a dry spot on the floor and felt around among empty boxes, discovering a large folded canvas, miraculously also dry. By this time I was very cold and water was running down my skin under my clothes. I decided to remove all my clothes and to partially unfold the canvas, lying on half and covering myself with the scratchy tickly other half. Already I had wrung out my clothing and spread out the soaked blanket, so I lay down in the canvas 'bed'. It was very cold there in the enclosed porch with the rain pouring outside and silence everywhere otherwise – a strange way to spend an evening. Then I started to massage myself from the feet right up to the very top of my head, where there was a very sore spot, then down again and up again. I kept up the massage as much as possible for the rest of the night, thus ensuring circulation. It was not possible to sleep due to the itchiness of the canvas, the crawling of strange insects, and the skin soreness produced by the constant rubbing.

So passed the hours. And in the dim light of early morning, I dressed in clothes still wet but not dripping. After a short time I heard movements in the house and store below. Collecting the blanket, the all-important fish, and the state papers, I emerged from my bedroom, carefully re-locking the door, and peered like a lost soul from some strange world at the kitchen entrance to the back of the house. The owner of the store saw me in the reflection from the electric light within. His eyes growing enormous in amazement and his face becoming pale, he called his wife, too overcome even to invite me in. Then the two of them, realizing who I was and my plight, hurried around, taking me into the warm kitchen and seating me with my back to the hot stove.

Strong coffee was prepared and a little cooking rum added. The contents of the cup were almost thrust down my throat to warm me from the inside. The man apologized for the rum saying that he and his wife both had dreadful colds. In an attempt to sweat them off, the night before they had prepared hot whiskey and lemon drinks, using up their last drop of whiskey. Then they had put themselves to bed and had become dead to the world, which included all my knocking.

When I was warm and dried off by the fire, and after my office in town was opened, the store owner phoned and told them that they should inform the road repair crew that when they found my empty car in between two rock slides – if it was still there – that I was safe and that he would take me by jeep to the scene of the action the night before.

The rain that morning had settled into a mild drizzle. So far the bridges had held up except for the one where half of the approach had disappeared into the river, leaving space only for jeeps, very small cars, and walkers. By noon the rock piles had been cleared enough for the car to pass.

There were no injuries to the vehicle, with the exception of one crushed wheel which was promptly replaced with a spare by the road workers. The leader of the road gang looked at me and said he had wondered where I was in that storm and if I was out on his roads. He just prayed that I would be spared. I was . . . and the blanket, the fish, (a little the worse for wear), the state papers, and myself, made our way back into town late that afternoon.

CHAPTER FIVE

Mrs Johnson's Other Vision

At the reservation they told me that Mrs Johnson lived in a small cottage in the middle of a large field down near the river. I was to follow Merwyn Lane past the poppies to the creek and turn left. A little way down this rutted lane I would see the field with the cottage in the distance and should be sure to close the gate after I entered, because the field was home for a herd of cows.

I did what I was told and, sure enough, there was a small cottage on the left, obviously not larger than one room with a tiny lean-to hanging on it. To the rear of the cottage there was a well, apparently dry, since this was summer, and the pail stood desolately upside down on the partially wrecked overhead beams of the pulley. Also at the back of the house and rather too close to the well was a privy, with two seat holes for companionship and the door hanging precariously by one hinge, making possible a full view of whoever was occupying the privy. I struggled with the gate into the field, finding it almost impossible to open, then decided to leave the car in the lane and walk to the cottage.

The building was very decrepit but had a small front porch set on supports leaning in several directions, and a wooden floor. I saw no signs of life in the cottage but was suddenly aware of a figure stretched out on the porch floor. For a moment I felt panic. The old lady must be dead, I thought. I crept closer with a sinking heart to see that she was fast asleep, lying on the bare boards, no cushion for her head or cover for her body. From her eyes there was a small, yellowish discharge (Mrs Johnson is blind, they had told me) and feasting on the mess were a number of flies. I looked in horror. What should I do? Should I disturb the flies, which would awaken her? Would such a move on my part frighten her? Or should I leave her to her uncomfortable and flyblown sleep, and return later? The decision was for returning, so I walked to my car in utter quiet.

When I got back Mrs Johnson was seated in a rickety, overstuffed chair on the porch. She greeted me, asked who I was and what I was doing there. Her eyes were now washed and the flies had departed. At one time she must have been a handsome woman, but was now shrunken, peering hopefully from obviously blind eyes. We talked. I told her my business, and she invited me into her cottage.

I noted that the lean-to was little more than a large cupboard for storage. Mrs Johnson skilfully built up the fire in an old metal stove and filled an antique copper teakettle with water dipped from a barrel. We waited for it to boil. 'Yes,' she said 'The well is dry. When the creek dries out, the well does too. But people are kind and bring me barrels of water almost every day from town.'

'How do you get food?' I asked.

'Oh, I walk to town and buy what I want in the store.'

Walk to town? I thought. Blind? I asked: 'How do you find your way?'

'You see, I have lived in this cottage most of my life, so I know the road and I know what direction it is in front. If it is a still day and there is no wind, I step outside, lick my finger and hold it up. Even if there is no wind there is always movement in the air, so I know which way to go. When I get to the gate, it's all easy after that.'

'How do you get back with a load of groceries?' I asked.

'Sometimes people give me a ride. You see,' she said, 'when you live a long time in a place it knows you and you know it, so all you have to do is find your wind and get started.'

I dared to ask: 'Are you happy alone in this wide field? Do you ever get frightened?'

She said: 'Yes, I am happy. Sometimes people come to see me, and in the bush near the house are small birds that sing to me, winter and summer. In winter I buy food for them, and they pay for it in summer song.'

No, she had no radio, but what was the news? It was always the same. I had noticed that the walls of the cottage were papered with old newspapers, some going back twenty years. No, she was not lacking news, twenty years ago or today.

Mrs Johnson was deep in the ways of horticulture. She rarely wore shoes and her large, tough-looking feet bore the marks of years of walking on rough ground. 'I like to feel the ground under my feet,' she said, 'and I know the flowers by the way they feel. No, I don't need cushions for my afternoon naps. I like the feel of the boards under me. You see, a tree is very strong and even when it is cut into boards the wood retains some of that strength – even when they are very old.'

I had to leave Mrs Johnson. As I began the long drive home from the reservation, my mind summed up what I had seen and heard. The lady I had visited was old, probably eighty-five. She lived in a one-room newspaper-lined cottage, clean but barely habitable. People visited her sometimes and the cows came. She could not see, but she could feel the grass under her feet and could tell the flowers by her toes. She had no radio but plenty of bird-song for music. She knew where and how to go when she needed to leave. In summer there was no water, but she could rely on friends to bring her enough. In her life Mrs Johnson had exchanged vision for feeling. She said she was happy, getting strength from the hard boards in her afternoon nap.

I thought about her as I drove, and of how my life had been enriched and perhaps could be simplified after knowing Mrs Johnson.

CHAPTER SIX

Roots – Lost and Found

I was told that when I went to interview Mr Ranki I might have to climb the gate to his little road. There was a wide place on the highway where I could leave the car and a small side gate might be unlocked. Mr Ranki liked to be left alone and was suspicious of all would-be visitors.

The warning was necessary. The big gate that would admit a car to the straggling, grass-grown road down to his house was locked very firmly, as was the small side entrance. I collected my papers, put them in the folder and climbed the gate. It was a rough path down, and I could hear the river below singing over rocks and into pools. There were flowers by the roadside and some interesting trees. I wondered if the occupant of the house I was visiting was a botanist at heart.

Suddenly the road turned a corner and I saw a small, one-room cabin. By the side of the house, a little to the rear, flowers were replaced by a large and unsightly heap of tin cans and empty whiskey bottles.

Preparing myself for what might be the worst, I knocked at the door. A husky voice called 'come in', so I lifted the latch and entered. The room was neat, containing on the far side a clean bed, a stove, a substantial table and a number of rather dilapidated chairs. There was also a chest of drawers with one or two photographs on top. Seated at the table was a ponderous man staring a little vacantly at a half-empty whiskey bottle. He glanced at me and seemed to be rather angry at my intrusion. Then, apparently noting that I was a woman carrying some papers, his whole attitude changed. Placing hands on the table he pushed himself up, straightened his strong heavily-built body, faced me, and made an elaborate salute with his right hand, his left one being placed over his heart. Bowing stiffly, Mr Ranki indicated that I should sit on one of the chairs and, still standing, asked my business. When I told him that I needed his signature on some papers that would give continuation of his pension he seemed very relieved.

His case history indicated that he had been born in Hungary. Gradually he relaxed and I asked how much he remembered of his life in the other country. He told me that he had been a captain in the Hungarian army, but that his son had emigrated to America and, after his wife died, he had followed the son into the new young land. He found American ways and people difficult, so he preferred to be alone. This was his son's property, he said, and he lived in the cabin as a sort of caretaker. From that story, of course, I recognized the standing salute when a woman entered – also the hand on the heart. Mr Ranki was wearing long, up-to-the-knee army boots, obviously European and old. They had once been very fine boots and were symbols of a former grandeur. He had quite a command of the English language, and informed me that officers were expected to have some knowledge of certain other European tongues.

I asked about the unusual flowers and trees along his entrance road. He told me that yes, the study of plants and the cultivation of rare specimens had always been one of his hobbies. How did he pass his time? He fished in the river, did quite a lot of reading, and worked with his plants. I inquired after his son and was told that the younger man rarely visited his father because he was ashamed of the older man's drinking habits. Mr Ranki missed his Hungarian lifestyle, his old friends, and even the army routine from which he had retired long ago. He wanted to show me the river and some of his flower beds. So, walking rather unsteadily, he led the inspection tour. It was time for me to leave, the return journey to the highway being slow because he insisted on accompanying me to the gates and unlocking the small one so that I would not have to climb.

Everything about this old man was ordered, dignified, and had a strange military precision. We said goodbye and again came the stiff salute and hand-over-heart. Then with a quick, almost official turn, he staggered off down the road to his lonely life.

America must have many men and women hidden away in lonely cottages who came to the country too late in life for proper adjustment. Why do they come? Some are following adult children who have settled in the new land. Some satisfy a fading sense of adventure – perhaps expecting that a new, young country will help restore some of their old lust for life.

Is their ending in a strange land, where customs are misunderstood and loneliness is a daily pattern, to be considered a tragedy? Or is it a mysterious sort of fulfilment, an adventure completed?

CHAPTER SEVEN

The Intruders

The Wiltshire ranch was along the railway tracks on the other side of the river from the road, so reaching it was quite a problem. There were alternatives. One could walk to it along the tracks to the bottom of the hill and then clamber up to the flattened area on which stood the house and the barn. This was quite a distance – perhaps two miles. The other approach was by travelling along the road to a point where the ranch was in view distantly on the opposite hill. The car was parked by the roadside and the journey to the house involved struggling down the rock-strewn river bank to the water's edge. Divested of shoes and stockings and with papers held safely in a briefcase, one selected a shallow place to wade across the river and then scrambled up the opposite bank, crossed the tracks and climbed up the hill to the farm. The river could be crossed only after a dry spell. So this method was used in the autumn – October or November – when the stream was at its lowest.

On a day in early November a visit to the Wiltshires' was due. Heavy rains had not yet commenced so I chose the water crossing as my method of approach. From where I parked the car I could look down at the water and speculate on its depth in areas where there were ruffles over the pebbly bottom. Sometimes that view could be deceptive but on this chosen day all appeared clear and passable.

After scrambling down the bank, sliding sometimes on slippery rocks, taking off shoes and stockings, and rolling skirts high, I entered the water at a point chosen by view from the road. On this day, however, the view was in a deceptive mood and the water turned out to be deeper over the ruffles than it appeared. The pebbles on the bottom were quite large and the crossing needed much attention in order to retain balance.

Suddenly, when I was about half-way across the stream, something large bumped into the back of my bare legs, almost knocking me over full length into the water. Arms flailing, I managed to recover and stay upright only to be bumped into again, this time with less threatening results. Bracing myself I stopped and looked down into the clear water. At that moment something that seemed slick and a little slimy slid past my left leg. The same thing happened to the right leg and then I saw the aggressors – a number of large steelhead swimming rapidly upstream, intent on their journey regardless of anything in their way. It was a strange feeling – these shiny bodies brushing against me and bent irrevocably to their objective.

Realizing that my feet were steadfastly planted and that I was safe from being knocked over, I remained still until I was sure that all the attackers had passed. When again secure I left the water, donned shoes and stockings, crossed the railroad tracks, and clambered up the bank to the farm.

I found Mr Wiltshire in bed sick, his wife worried lest they should need a doctor. I reassured Mrs Wiltshire that her husband was not sick enough to require medical attention and then told them my fish story. The husband was immediately alert and seemed at the point of instant recovery: 'Alice, go and get my fishing tackle from the shed. I should be out there getting us some fish.' We dissuaded him with difficulty and when he tried to stand up he realized that his influenza settled the matter. Through guessing rather than knowledge I told another fish story to the effect that today's steelhead had passed but that if he was well enough tomorrow to go down to the river another group might be passing.

Finishing my business I returned down the hill from the ranch, crossed the railroad, and again entered the water, hoping that my guess was correct and the fish encounter would not be repeated. Fortunately for me the only intruders I saw on my return trip through the water were my own two feet on the pebbly river bottom.

CHAPTER EIGHT

Love in the Forest

Louis Augier lived in a small cabin far back in the woods that had been logged perhaps fifty years ago. The area had been neglected so there were many young trees, fortunately not quite ready for harvesting, and a large number of stumps from the last cutting. At the time of the previous harvest the stumps were taller than those in the present harvesting period, since cutting tools had been less sophisticated some fifty years ago.

The road to the cabin was a long-deserted logging track, usually impassable after rain. To be careful, I left the car on a better part of the road and walked towards the small house.

As I approached I was met by a dog and a cat walking side by side, stepping gingerly and suspiciously, both tails stiff and bristly as if with apprehension, the tail of the cat straight up in the air and that of the dog stuck out rigidly behind him. I spoke to them assuring them of my worthiness, and they turned together as if in lock-step and marched ahead of me, side by side, to the cabin. I noticed a large heap of empty whiskey and wine bottles towards the rear of the house and prepared myself for what might be the worst.

A thin elderly man, who seemed rather pale and a little ill, emerged from the house and greeted me. His two guardians, reassured that I was all right, tails smooth and down, found a shady spot and settled down to sleep together. I remarked that his two friends took good care of him and Mr Augier agreed, adding that when he had taken 'a drop too much' they followed him everywhere, never letting him out of their sight in case he needed help.

I explained to Mr Augier the reason for my visit. I had been told that he was ill and might need transportation to town and a doctor. As I talked my eyes wandered over the area surrounding the cabin. To my astonishment it was covered with every kind of tin can holding baby trees; even the tall stumps of long harvested redwoods had small trees planted in the rotting material at the top of the stumps. There must have been a hundred of these babies, all obviously tenderly cared for and watered.

Mr Augier noted my surprise and explained that he loved the little trees and that from time to time, as they matured, he planted them in other parts of the forest so that there would always be trees. 'You see,' he said simply, 'I love them.'

This indeed was an area of love. The cat and dog loved one another. Obviously they loved and cared for the man with whom they lived and he in turn appreciated them. The very air he breathed was filled with love of this strange man for his baby trees.

Mr Augier would not go to town with me. He was feeling better and who would water his trees and care for them if he had to stay overnight? We talked a little about the trees and I admired and praised his care. When I turned to leave, Mr Augier picked up a healthy youngster in a two-pound coffee can and gave it to me. I protested, saying that he would miss his little friend and that it would be lonely without the other trees. He told me I must talk to it, give it care and love, and it would grow for me. I placed the can carefully in the back of the car, said goodbye to the three loving friends, and left that gentle area.

Some weeks later the county nurse again asked me if I would look in on Mr Augier the next time I was near his cabin. She had heard that he was again very unwell. Once more I was greeted by the suspicious cat and dog but this time accepted more readily. Mr Augier seemed a little more feeble than on my first visit but refused transportation to town and a doctor.

Once more I was presented with another baby tree in another coffee can. I refused, saying that he had already given me one tree and that was enough. 'Oh no, it was not enough, because if there were two trees, they would talk together and be happier.' So again I loaded the tree into the car, paid my respects, and left the love area.

Several months passed before there was a call for another visit to Mr Augier. On this occasion he was really quite ill and willing to to to town with me to see the doctor, if he could get back the same day to care for his friends.

As before I was presented with another small tree which I refused, saying that the first two were happy and talking to one another. 'Ahh, no,' he said. 'If you take a third tree there will be a great, big, happy chatter.' So again I loaded a little tree into my car and this time included my loving friend.

Looking back on the little home I saw the cat and dog standing together, guarding the house, looking very puzzled. What would happen to them? What would happen to all the little trees if, as seemed likely from his present appearance, Mr Augier could never return? A lump tightened in my throat and tears threatened.

'The cat and dog will look after the house,' said Mr Augier. 'Everything will be all right until I come back tonight.'

CHAPTER NINE

The Scalped Head

I had a very tall friend who was also a publisher. In addition to those two qualifications, he was very interested in Indian culture. He was aware of the fact that through my work I was closely involved with many of the Indian people. Mr Greene had written several books about Indians and their philosophy. I'm ashamed to say that I had not read his books, knowing very well what the average white writer thinks he knows about the average Indian.

Mr Greene lived some distance away but wrote and asked if he could accompany me on some occasion when I would meet several Indians. Or, if I was going to the reservation, could he go with me and explore the country and possibly be introduced to an Indian family? This I could not do unless I had permission.

After I gained that permission we set off very early one morning. I noticed that he placed in the back of my car two large and heavy pasteboard boxes. This was none of my business, so I did not comment on them.

Since the day would be long and rather arduous I decided to go first to the reservation and satisfy Mr Greene's curiosity. The road up into the mountains was (and still is) quite thrilling, with magnificent views from the higher levels down into the deep gorges where a turbulent river flowed noisily. It is not an easy road to drive and, in the earlier days of my work, was sometimes impassable for short periods. Landslides made every journey a questionable pilgrimage. On the day of Mr Greene's visit all was calm and serene with many flowers, snow still clinging to the higher peaks, and ornamental cumulus clouds playing games with the sunlight. Mr Greene was almost overcome by the beauty of these new surroundings.

On reaching my destination I stopped at two houses where the visits were brief – not concerned with the government business, but long enough for me to introduce the visitor to two Indian families.

Then we moved cross-country for more than a mile to a pleasant house situated in an over-grazed meadow. Here I stayed to conduct my business, leaving Mr Greene in the car. My interview completed, I asked permission of the resident of the house for an introduction for Mr Greene. The hostess was a very alert lady and quite willing to talk. After the introduction and a very short period of general conversation, Mr Greene excused himself, saying that he wished to show the hostess two books on Indians to see if she would care to read them. He left us alone and the lady of the house gave me a very sly look, saying 'I wonder what it is *this* time,' and I replied that I had no idea about the presence of books and that he had merely asked for transportation and for an introduction to a few people.

The house in which we were visiting had been built many years ago for his young wife by the lady's husband and was very superior to most of the cottages, even boasting sanitation, and kitchen and bathroom facilities. Both of the occupants, however, had been short people and the front porch running the length of the house was low.

Mr Greene returned, carrying one of the pasteboard boxes I had noted when we left on the journey. As he approached the cottage from the car he crashed his head into the low beam of the porch. The wound was bleeding a little when he entered but he made no fuss about it and started immediately to open the box which, to my horror, disclosed a number of books of his own publication. He took out one or two of these and handed them to his victim/hostess. He explained that the books were about Indians and Indian philosophies and said that he hoped she would read them and find them to be correct in substance and in detail. Then he added the price of the books. The lady gave me a glance unobserved by Mr Greene which almost said, 'What did I tell you?' I smiled back understanding her look. The lady then said that she could not possibly afford the books since she was a widow and a pensioner, so he must try to dispose of them to a more knowledgeable person. She handed the books back to him, went into her kitchen, opened the refrigerator and returned with an ice pack for Mr Greene to apply to his scalp wound.

I was anxious to get away from there as quickly as possible to avoid any further discussion of books. I told Mr Greene we had to leave as I had many other calls to make. He repacked his box, carrying it under one arm while holding the ice pack on the cut on his head with his free hand.

The lady of the house apologized for the low beam of her porch, adding that she rarely had such tall visitors. Then she asked him: 'On the occasion of your first visit to the reservation, doesn't it seem strange that you should be scalped by an Indian?'

Unhappily I had to inform the scalped gentleman that he would not again try to sell his books from a government car. For safety's sake I decided it would be better not to try for more visits and introductions with the Indians. I then told Mr Greene that we would finish the work on the reservation perhaps on another date, but that now I must return to the highway and complete other visits to different types of homes where he could retain his scalp.

CHAPTER TEN

Roses

Walter Gillespie was an alcoholic. He denied the fact quite fiercely, saying that he could stop drinking at any time and stay off the stuff. It was true that when pressured he could go 'on the wagon' for a few days. At these times he would sit around nursing a bottle of coke and looking thoroughly miserable. Always after a few days of non-drinking he returned to his normal habits.

Walter had been married, but after the birth of three boys and a girl his wife divorced him and requested custody of the children. Strangely enough, however, as soon as the boys were old enough to select the parent they wished to live with, the boys all came to the father. Even the youngest, who had not yet attained the age of selection, was constantly running away from the mother and joining his older brothers with the father. I wondered about this fact and felt that it must disclose some hidden goodness in Walter.

The older boys were twins, quiet, well-behaved, good students and on the point of graduating into high-school. Walter made his living in various ways, but principally by the operation of his large truck with which he would do hauling. That, of course, meant that when he was not actually working with the truck he had a great deal of time just to sit around waiting for orders.

The boys took infinite care of Walter. As soon as school was over they looked for him, found him, and spent their evenings with him doing their homework – but always there was a watchful eye on the older man. When Walter received orders that would take him and the truck some distance away from town, the boys always took a day off from school and accompanied him. It was almost a reversal of the parent/child position, the boys having become the caretaker of the father, who this way kept out of serious trouble arising from his drinking. Both boys were expert operators of the truck. Local police winked their eyes at the fact that the twins were under driving age. No doubt they felt that under-age safe drivers were preferable to a drunken one. As soon as the boys thought that their father had had enough, they loaded him into the truck and drove him home. The family owned a small, dilapidated ranch with a ranch house. They kept a few head of growing cattle they bought at sales, nursed and fed into maturity, and then sold at a profit. I was told that the boys did most of the work with the young stock.

As the time of graduation approached the twins became quite excited. Rarely had they been anywhere for entertainment, and even the local movies were largely unknown to them. As is the way in most schools, regulations for the dance were a little stupid and limiting. The girls could wear their pretty dresses but the boys had to wear black or dark trousers and immaculate white shirts. For the poorer families this posed a problem. The twins had no respectable white shirts. They were invited to join some young friends with their parents for a lift to the dance. But without shirts that would be useless.

Walter remembered that he had some money due from work

finished the week before the dance. So he promised the boys that immediately upon receiving the money he would buy them a white shirt each. Unfortunately Walter had to drive to the neighbouring town to collect his money. As usual, the boys took a day off from school and accompanied him. Walter collected his money, but on the way to the store for the shirts again misfortune treated him badly. He met a man he had not seen for a number of years, and by way of celebration of the meeting they stepped across to 'have one'. The one led to many. Soon most of the money had gone and there were no shirts. Again Walter was drunk, so the boys loaded him into the truck and drove him home.

The following day I noticed the sickly father and two very unhappy boys. I also noticed that they never chastised or grumbled about the older man for his misdeeds. For them it was part of life, always had been, and probably always would be.

I could not bear the thought of the two boys robbed of the one pleasure they would have for a long time. I asked Walter if there were any dirty old white shirts that could be washed and used. He doubted that, but said he would go and look. He left for home and later reappeared carrying two most horrible dirty white shirts. He said: 'These are all they have, and I think they are so far gone that you could do nothing with them.'

In spite of his warning, however, I took the filthy specimens and left them to soak for a while in hot sudsy water. Then I visited the local grocery store to see if they had any stain remover. All they had were bottles of stuff to remove grass stains. I took that and returned to the house and the filthy horrors. Several washings restored the garments to a stained semblance of their former whiteness. I then worked on the stains. After further re-washing and a little starch, the shirts appeared passable. Carefully ironed they really were not bad at all. I found two identical boxes and some blue tissue paper. Placing the shirts in their new homes, I took the boxes to town.

This was the morning of the graduation dance and Walter was, as usual, sitting at the bar and two sad-faced boys were munching hamburgers. I presented each one with a box, the whiteness gleaming through the blue paper. The boys had a strange look in their eyes that I almost interpreted as tears. Leaving their unfinished supper they rushed off to wash and change. Later I saw them getting into the car with their friends to go off to the graduation dance. Apparently the party went well. The village seemed to be happy and satisfied.

There was no word from Walter and his sons until the following Tuesday when, in the evening when I was at home, I heard a knock at my door. I found that it was Walter carrying a very large, slightly greasy, brown paper shopping bag. He handed the bag to me saying: 'These are for you for the shirts. I want to thank you very much. The boys also wish to convey their thanks, but as you know, they are very shy. So I am doing it for them. They had a simply wonderful time.'

I peeked inside the slightly unsavoury bag and there found an enormous spray of old-fashioned red cottage roses – the sort of rose where even the buds are full of promise and the perfume is out of this world. I was speechless and turned to thank Walter. But he had left and was walking down the path from my house to the road.

Automatically I noted his walk. It was straight, crisp, and unfumbled. He was obviously completely sober.

CHAPTER ELEVEN

Service Around the Catacombs

Early on Friday morning I received a telephone call. It was from Miriam, one of the many women I knew who had severe and unexplained problems. She was crying into her telephone: I could feel the tears. She asked if I could come immediately to see her and help with a burial. Through the tears I gathered that one of her twenty-two member cat family had died. Merky (short for Mercury) had been a very old cat, a long-time friend of Miriam, so incredibly thin during his past two years that if he were picked up, or if he jumped on laps for comfort, he had the feel of a fur-covered ghost hanging limply like a stole over the arm of his holder. I had to explain to Miriam that I would be working in another district that day, and therefore unable to reach her cottage, which was in a distant village. I assured her that I would make a special trip on Saturday to see what I could do to help.

Miriam was a strangely unhappy woman, lonely by both condition and choice although intellectually brilliant. She sought comfort in her loneliness by collecting stray cats. These animals were pampered to an extreme degree, never leaving the house, performing all their affairs in the building with aromas best not described.

On Saturday morning I gathered some groceries, firewood, and sawdust from the mill to take over to the unhappy woman. I found Miriam, now tearless and full of plans, regarding with grief the motionless body of Merky. The dead cat lay on a prized silk scarf such as would be suitable for the dead body of royalty. I found that I was to dig a hole under a favourite tree. Miriam herself, a hypochondriac, verging at times on alcoholism, could not attempt the heavy digging among the tough roots of the redwood.

Finally, puffing and panting, I dropped my grubbing hoe from blistered hands and remarked that it had to be deep enough. Prized scarf and Merky were tenderly wrapped in soft paper and placed in a pasteboard box which in turn was covered by more attractive cloths and lowered into the grave. Wild flowers were gathered and placed over the 'coffin'. We joined hands and together, on instructions from Miriam, prayed for the soul and happy landing in whatever was the heaven of the deceased animal. Quietly I took my shovel and replaced the earth, covering Merky forever.

By this time Miriam had collapsed through her grief and could no longer help even with earth shovelling. I thought the funeral was over, but no! I was instructed to walk around the grave, my hand in her hand, muttering prayers and singing hymns. In some way this eerie service affected me so that the reality of the affair in which I'd been involved escaped and I found myself to be almost a part of the soul of the vanished old cat. More flowers were gathered and scattered on and around the fresh dirt. At this point I turned towards the house and noted many pairs of apparently astonished eyes gazing through a window that overlooked the redwood tree and the grave site. Then I realized that Miriam had built steps inside the room up to the window ledge, so that the remaining members of her cat family could also watch the entombment of one of their members.

Perhaps the widely staring eyes broke the spell of the ritualistic funeral and I returned to normal living, realizing that the scene and action of which I had so recently been a part were an incongruity and almost a sacrilege. And yet . . . ? If there are souls in a cat system, who was to be a little shocked by the event? Also I realized that I could not, indeed must not, condemn Miriam who was obviously at extremes in her loneliness, regarding her animal kingdom as efficient substitutes for human companionship.

After the 'ceremony' was over I stayed with Miriam for a little while, driving her out along country lanes in the bright afternoon sunshine to partly dispel her gloom. On my way home I found myself adding another prayer to the soul, if any, of the departed creature – that in my end I would remain able to converse and pray with humankind and not be left exposed in bitter loneliness to the ritualistic burial of a loved animal.

CHAPTER TWELVE

Baby Blue Eyes

It was almost forty miles from the highway to Merelow up in the mountains; the dirt road is rough, narrow, winding, and nearly deserted. At first the lane is fairly level, following the river, making occasional sudden leaps over the high bluffs, limbering up maybe for the long climb ahead. Except for a few ranch trucks, one's fellow travellers may be straying cattle, deer, a skunk or two, a fox and, down by the water, grey-feathered fishermen standing humped over long legs in the sunlight, watching deep pools.

It is a beautiful road, high rocky ledges on one side and, on the other, the river slipping greenly between brightly coloured boulders or bursting into a white flutter of frills at the neck of a waterfall. Spring and summer have their flowers and on frosty autumn days bright red Toyon berries glow warmly. In winter snow lies softly on the high slopes.

But from experience it is not a road to be stranded on; one can so easily spend the night there. So it was a little worrying that I had not yet found the turn I sought. The turn was one mile north of Buck Rock, directions read, and about a half mile south of Kelly

Creek – a steep lane with a barbed wire gate. But at that point there was no lane, no gate, only a 'slip out' of the road.

I retraced to Buck Rock where I noticed a home-made sign nailed to a post: an arrow with the word 'TRAL' painted on it, and the name 'JOHN PAX'.

Pax – Peace! I could do with some.

Perhaps Mr Pax could give me more specific directions. Parking the car, I followed the pointing arrow down a steep 'tral' towards the river. Here was a canopy of leafy branches making a deep green tunnel, cool, shadow-patterned, flowery, and refreshing as a breeze on this hot June afternoon. On the high grassy bank there were many flowers: columbines, ferns, fiddle-heads, blue star, hound tongues, larkspur, birthday-candles of buckeye and, near a spring, a spray of late-flowering 'baby blue eyes', locally so-named, so pale and soft tinted that the colour seemed washed out by recent rains.

The spring water tinkled delicately into a neat round pool and was delicious, tasting of earth and flowers, sunlight, and secret places of underground.

The trail opened suddenly into a clearing that sloped to the river. There was a vegetable garden inside a very high wire fence and a tiny cabin. Stove-length wood was piled neatly all along by one wall of the cottage under the eaves. An old man was tearing down the pile of wood, moving it into a rough heap exposing the wall. He did not hear or see me.

'Good evening,' I called.

He straightened up, leaving his work, and returned the greeting. Here was the mildest looking face I had ever seen, and the most wrinkled. Pale blue eyes, soft, washed out like the baby blue eyes near the spring, gazed out of a network of deep criss-crossed wrinkles and folds. It was a thin sun-tanned face, with sparse, greying, brown hair on his head. When he spoke his voice was so soft, so quiet as to be almost a whisper. The whole effect was of a person *drained*, dehydrated body and soul emptied of emotions.

'I didn't hear you. I'm moving this wood from in front of a hole to under the house. A mother cat had kittens in here last week. She was killed on the road this morning and I buried her; now the kittens must be got out and fed or they will die.'

Obviously it was the natural thing, the only thing to do, so he did it. He returned to the log moving and I helped. Soon the opening to under the house was big enough and he crawled into the dark place, emerging a few moments later with three helplessly squirming babies, vaguely opening small pink mouths, eyes tight shut. They were gently placed in a box on some newspapers, little heads hopefully twisting this way and that, seeking the buried mother.

'I can feed them with rags dipped in milk, and when they are good and hungry they will suck the rags,' Mr Pax explained.

The only thing that worried him was whether when they grew up, and of course they *would* grow up, the kittens might attack and eat his pet chipmunks. Perhaps if they grew up *with* the chipmunks, they would all get along together. We both hoped for this. Mr Pax gazed wistfully at his squirming family.

'It is nice here. You have a fine garden.'

He agreed that it was nice. But as for the garden, this would be its last year. The high fence kept the big deer out, but the little fawns sometimes got their heads fast in the wire mesh; he would hear them crying just before daylight and have to get up and set them free. 'And sometimes the skin on their necks is cut by the wire, and that is bad,' he said.

Kittens, chipmunks, baby deer – everything about him so gentle, meek, unevil, almost breathlessly anxious to *care* about what was in distress.

I told him my troubles, and asked about the turn I had missed.

'The road slipped out yesterday and has buried the gate. You will have to go further north up Riley Lane. Keep on the rocks at the sludge hole and turn right by the fence.' I thanked him and helped carry the box of kittens to the house.

In his cottage it was unbelievably orderly and neat. An elderly black stove and a large iron bed took up most of the floor space. There was room only for a table and two chairs with backs, and one without a back which was the wash-stand. It held a clean tin bowl turned upside down, some soap in a chipped saucer and a towel. Sunday trousers and a white shirt hung on a nail on the wall. I sat down for a moment and listened to the soft whispering voice and the quiet whoosh of the river outside.

Answering my questions he said that he lived alone, had a little pension. Years ago he had owned six horses and drove the mail over Blain Pass between Alderly and Dean – two days in and two days out. 'Them was the days, but it was bad in winter,' he said. 'Now the roads is better and it is all truck work. A horse man can't get work no more, but horses is best, they're friendly.'

I stood up to leave and suddenly saw it! Under the chair that had stood by the wall in a dark corner – a terrifying, grimacing, demoniacal face, staring at me – through me – out of the gloom. Mr Pax followed my horrified gaze.

'That's only my head,' he said, and moved over to draw the monstrous thing from the corner.

His head! Never! This gentle old man and this grimacing thing of horror – definitely no relationship. Mr Pax regarded his sculptured masterpiece with warm pride.

'I carved it a while ago out of a piece of ironstone from down by the river. It took me well over a year, the rock was so hard. Them's hog tussies.'

'Them' were long hog tusks, protruding from the corners of the mouth, curving up towards glinting, prominent eyes set in deep sockets. In the eyes was a hopeless, unknowing primitive fear; the 'tussies' belied the fear with a hint of fierce brutality. From earlobes and nose hung pieces of bone. The mouth was exquisitely moulded; full sensual lips, slightly parted, showed long sharp cruel teeth – more 'hog tussies' no doubt. Here, in a ghastly life-size form, was a gathering of all that is meanest, lowest, and most primitive in human emotions – a mockery of 'in the beginning'. I glanced at his creation.

'Why do you keep it?'

'It's company for me,' he said.

'COMPANY!'

I looked closer. It was a beautifully modelled head, worked by the hands of an artist and rubbed to a shining smoothness. The chin was firm and round; ears over-large but true. There were no wasted cuts, there was no fuss – only a Rodin-like clarity and economy of line. 'I like to look at him,' the soft voice continued. 'There's times when I think he is the bad part of me. It's like if you could pull your sins out and look at them, you'd see how ugly they are, and you'd be frightened and stay good.'

To tear out of himself all that is evil and then sit alone regarding it. What a pastime!

Not many people had seen it, he said. One man offered him seventy-five dollars, but Mr Pax liked his 'company' – his disembodied sins – more than he needed the money. No, he had never carved anything before or since, and no one told him how. No, he had no picture to follow and no book to read and did not know much about reading or writing. He used an old screwdriver for a chisel and another rock for a hammer. Later he had found a file and that helped.

It was getting late. Through the window I could see long tongues of shadow licking the foothills, tasting the night. We left the 'company' in the middle of the floor and went outside into the fading sunlight.

'Do you like flowers? I will pick you some.' The whispered voice murmured and the mild face beamed gently. He gathered a gay bouquet – columbine, wild larkspur, and hounds' tongue, gave it to me and smiled a quiet goodbye.

'Don't forget to mind the sludge hole,' he said.

Up the green tunnel of a trail and back to the car, I laid the bouquet on the seat and there, nodding gently beside me, was the spray of baby blue eyes.

CHAPTER THIRTEEN

The White Lily

Have you seen but a white lily grow,
Before rude hands have touched it?
Have you marked but the fall of the snow,
Before the earth has smutched it?
Have you felt the wool of the beaver,
Or swan's down ever,
Or have smelt of the bud of the briar
Or the nod in the fire?
Or have tasted the bag of the bee?
Oh so white! Oh so soft! Oh so sweet is she.

Ben Jonson

In the valley at 'Jack's Place' the coffee is good, the pea soup is out of this world and the gossip always succulent, so everyone stops there. On this day I called as usual to sample all three. Greeting the lunchtime group, deep in a discussion, I was at once included.

Did I know Old Dominic Welsky up in the hills above Ely? I knew him by repute and was not anxious for further contact. Why, was there trouble?

It seems that when Ed Dean rode past the Welsky place after cattle, he saw the old man chopping wood and hardly able to walk. It looked as if he'd had an accident recently, cutting his leg pretty badly, and the untended wound had turned on him. It was swollen, Ed said, and the old man looked sick. Ed offered to stay and clean the wound, but the old man wouldn't have him near the cabin and sent him away.

Everyone knew about Dom; crazy as a loon they said, wouldn't have a road to his shack and lived alone, refusing to let anyone inside his property. Naturally tales grew and squandered themselves around the valley; there were stories about what was hidden in the cabin. Gold some said; others claimed more gruesome things. Dom came years ago from Austria and still had a queer accent and foreign ways. But those who knew him better, those who stopped at the gate and talked, liked Old Dom in a way. Some said he had soft brown eyes but they never looked *at* you, just through you to the hills or somewhere, never really seeing you.

He was kind, too, if you kept your distance, giving presents of berries, wild honey and eggs from his half-dozen hens. But he got angry if you tried to go near the cabin. At Jack's they asked would I walk up and see if I could persuade Old Dom to let me dress his hurt leg. This idea was particularly unpleasant, even alarming, since no one really knew the old man and there was small hope of success. But after years of working in those hills, one always went when asked, or if there was trouble.

If you are scared, someone will go with you, they said. But, they added, it would be best to go alone.

One of the men gave directions to the Harwell Ranch — ten miles up the road — where Mr Harwell would indicate the rest of the way to the Welsky cabin. Park the car and walk up the canyon a short distance. Then I would wade the creek, climb a mile or so to a split oak, and from there follow a dim trail marked by a few blazed trees.

Finishing soup, coffee and apple pie, I paid and set off for the Harwell Ranch. Mr Harwell took me to a small bluff behind the barns and pointed out the white line of the split oak, showing faintly on a distant hill. It would be a tough walk, he said, and he doubted if I could do anything for Old Dom, especially since I was a woman. No woman had been seen there for almost twenty years.

It was indeed a tough walk carrying the First Aid Kit. There was no path; one kept the general direction in mind and clambered on up the slope, slippery with brown summer grass. It was not, still and drowsy in the afternoon sun, confusing to follow the slight track. The cabin certainly was remote. I reached an old rickety picket fence surrounding some buildings, and there at a gate stood Old Dom, a ridiculous figure in baggy trousers, far too large, tied up with a string. His worn hands, bony and criss-crossed with knotted ropes of veins, grasped the fence; broken spectacles bobbed on his nose, trying to part company, slowly sliding off the end. He looked sick.

'Vot you vont here? You can go no more.'

I explained my mission, trying to sound casual – perhaps I could do something to help his leg? I was a sort of nurse; it would only take a few minutes and we could work outside if he preferred. I looked anxiously at the old man who gazed through and beyond me, not seeing.

'No, you can do nussing. It vill get vell, maybe. Already it smell better.'

Persuasion had no effect. It was like talking to the winds; something not really there. It was silly. Hot, angry and defeated, I turned round and started home. A noise made me look back. Dom had unlatched the gate, his eyes on me, staring, seeing me for the first time. I met that unblinking gaze, and we stood so for a full half-minute. Clasping hands over his head, suddenly he shouted: 'E-e-e-e!' Strange and terrifying, the quiet old man exploded into the violence of a half-scream, half-laugh, startling me.

He hooked a bony finger, beckoning. Trying not to let the raw edges of my nerves show, I followed. The cabin was strong and squat, low and cosy, built of whole logs, the cracks plastered with mud. Plants grew in the muddied cracks, creating a garden standing on end. Hand-split shingles made the roof; hand-cut doors led into the woodshed and kitchen.

Inside it was cool and clean. I looked around at the big roof beams, shelves loaded with boxes of old china and several teapots. There were homemade chairs with high seats and backs, a heavy table with fat legs, an old black stove and plants in the window – everything so clean, bright and a little foreign, duskily gay like a Rembrandt interior.

'You vont coffee? I make coffee.' Still watching me, he stirred the fire, putting on more wood, and moved a large teakettle over the flame. I met his gaze.

'You small and qvick, qvick like a squirrel, you have vhite pale skin, pale hair like hers but not gold anymore. And you are not so vhite, but qvick. She was so . . . so . . .' He searched for a word but did not find it, and gazed away unseeingly. Suddenly 'E-e-e-e-e-e!' sounded again, the hands clasped above his head and the explosion of scream and laughter, excited. Grasping the edge of the table, I held on.

'She vas my vife. She die tventy year ago. They take her avay, down the mountain in a vheelbarrow. She go, but part she stay and someday she vill come back just the same. I vait for her. I let no one come here so she vill not be frightened. I think maybe you – you – but you are not, only qvick qvick like her, but *older*!'

He stared again, watching me; the kettle beginning a slow,

whispered song. 'Yah! She vas beautiful. So – you are not beautiful no more.' (Well, I thought, twenty years ago *I* was not so bad looking either, and twenty years younger.) He continued in a sing-song voice: 'She was so gently and soft and sveet, gently and sveet like a flower, so vhite, and gold in her hair. Come!'

Eyes luminous with memory, he crooked his finger again, and I followed into a dim bedroom. There were two beds, an old heavy quaint double bed with posts, and a cot. The big bed was made up for sleeping and was covered with a quilt. It might have been slept in last night – it could be waiting for tonight, except for the dust. There were *inches* of dust on the posts, the quilt – everywhere. Underneath was an old chamber pot, wreathed with a pattern of ivy leaves, deep in dust like the bed. On an old sewing machine at the foot was a knitted shawl and on the shawl a crocheted mat. On the mat stood a glass vase with long-dead flowers, all deep in dust, in soft grey dust like a shroud.

The cot was fresh, clean with a bright quilt, and the floor underneath, the bed rails and the chamber pot, were all immaculate. Obviously it was now the old man's bed. I reached my hand out to touch the flowers lightly. There is something so very pathetic about flowers dead in a vase. Dominic Welsky snatched my arm away, angry.

'Don't touch! They vere hers. Everything hers like she put them before she die, tventy year ago.'

Almost twenty years of memorial dust! I looked at the old man gazing at the flowers I had so nearly desecrated. Strangely, he no longer seemed ridiculous, a figure of fun. He was magnificent. The room was filled with a warm glow of tenderness and beauty. For an instant I was caught in a strange and lovely light, something beyond life. The kettle protested noisily, breaking the moment, and we left that divided room.

In the kitchen he made coffee which we drank from cracked cups, and he let me clean and dress his leg, scarcely noticing. It was bad, but not hopeless. I showed him how to change the dressing and said I could come back in two weeks.

All the time I worked he questioned. Could I milk? I could. Did I sew? Yes I did. Did I know about goats? 'She had lovely little goats – kept them for pets.' Yes, I too had goats. In deep, something of the spirit of the past must be in me! There were home-cured hides everywhere in the cabin. 'She' had cured them. Hides made rugs, chair seats and wall hangings. I admired them.

Coffee and leg finished, Dom led me outside to an old barn. Stretched over a saddle beam were half-a-dozen old goat hides, once beautiful, now dusty, covered with the fragile shells of discarded moth homes. Four of these old hides, reverently dusted, were wrapped in faded yellow newspapers and handed to me in triumph. I must take them because I was like her. He was really giving me a part of himself.

'Why don't you ask people to your cabin? Let them see the things she made and the home she lived in? Tell them about her? Isn't it rather unkind and selfish to keep her all to yourself like this?'

That was a new idea and he thought about it. He would think more, he said, and let me know when I came again. '*You* tell them about her,' he said.

Picking up my case and the unsavoury hides, I left on the long walk back.

Old Dom watched me go, brown eyes lit by the paling evening light, luminous, lovely. Next time, I told myself, I would bring the hides back, dig a grave near the cabin and bury them. They belonged on the land she had worked and loved.

There was no next time. Ten days later a crazed person

wandering over the hills found Dominic's cabin and shot the old man. They took his body down the mountain in a wheelbarrow.

In my outside shed is a bundle of old goat hides. Each spring-cleaning I throw them out to burn, but somehow they find their way back. Little soft moths still hatch out and flit into my house, like flecks of grey memorial dust.

CHAPTER FOURTEEN

Mountain Lion

Visits to the Mack Ranch were quite an undertaking. There were six or seven gates to open and close, the closing being very important lest the cattle from one ranch stray on to a neighbour's property or, worse still, on to the highway. It was quite a long drive from town into the hills and the ranch country. Many of the homesteads were now abandoned as agricultural projects but were used as residences for elderly retired couples.

This was the situation of the Mack family. Their children had been raised on the farm but were now gone to town and into various successful occupations. Mr and Mrs Mack remained on their acreage, but, apart from a few chickens, a hog, and two horses, they had no further interest in farming.

Once one had managed the many gates, the road degenerated somewhat and climbed into semi-forested country. On the day of my visit I had passed into the forested area where the road was rough but passable for the car. I wondered why an elderly couple would choose to live on property so remote when they could have moved into a town.

After about a mile in the forest I realized that the road had deteriorated into dry mud wheel-tracks with high centres, promising disaster if the car slipped into the deep ruts, so I decided to park, and walk the remaining mile or so to the house.

It was a beautiful walk with many flowers in the open parts of the forest and a few fine old trees. Without warning the lane veered a little to the left. And there ahead of me, crossing the road slinkily, was a very large mountain lion. The curve in the road ahead of me meant that I had been unable to see him until he was too near for comfort.

We had both stopped instantly, staring each at the other. He was magnificent, with a fine silken coat and clear young eyes. As he stood he had one paw raised as if interrupted in the act of walking. We continued staring, apparently neither one of us knowing quite what to do. Suddenly he hissed loudly and bounded away into the forest. I did not exactly hiss, but seeing the road ahead of me clear I hurried away from this spot.

Soon after my encounter with the lion, the road opened, revealing long distances of pasture country that sloped gently down into a fascinating blue distance.

There, a little below me, was the farm house, well built, with very orderly surroundings. My appearance was greeted by three large dogs who informed the occupants of the house that there might be danger about. A man appeared at the door of the house, spoke to them quietly, and with one more glance at me the dogs retired to tend to their own business.

Mr and Mrs Mack greeted me very kindly and inquired about my journey, noting that I had walked from the forest hill above them. They considered that wise because it was all too easy for a passenger car to be hung up on a high centre in the road. I, in turn, told them about the mountain lion. They said they knew all about him but were not alarmed. So far he had left them alone: not even a chicken was missing. The dogs were very well trained and even a young mountain lion in his prime would hesitate to encounter three dogs. Two of the dogs, he said, were old hands at the game and knew exactly what to do. The third was young and a student being trained by the older dogs.

The house was simply but charmingly funished in a style that was almost Victorian. From the window of the comfortable living room one looked out upon at least a half mile of soft green, park-like meadows with occasional fine old trees giving shelter and shade to any stock that might be feeding there. With the protecting forest behind, the long soft fields in front of the house, and the orderly farm buildings, I began to understand why the old couple chose to remain in the house they had originally established and in which they had raised their children.

After we had completed the business which was the cause of my visit we sat and talked for a little while. They were interested in what I could tell them of life in the small town, but remarked that they wanted none of it. I questioned about the mountain lion. Were they nervous on their own behalf and, should their grandchildren visit, what would they do?

Mr Mack said that when grandchildren came they were always accompanied (if they strayed from the house) by one or two dogs so he held no fears. As for his wife and himself they felt perfectly safe and it was a matter of live and let live. After all, he said, mountain lions, bears, and such animals had enjoyed the rights of this country long before the white man established farms. Now it was a matter of sharing and, as long as the wildlife kept its boundaries, the intruding farmers could have no complaints.

They had always loved their home, he said, and although getting the ranch established had been very hard work, it had been a joyous time with the arrival and growing up of children around them. He asked me if I didn't think it would be foolish for them to leave this spot where they had enjoyed beauty and a full family life, to move into some city or town where living would be cramped and days empty. Naturally I agreed with him, being a countrywoman myself.

With one long last look around me at this pastoral scene I prepared to leave. Mr Mack said that for safety's sake he did not want me to walk back to the car, so he brought out a jeep from its shed in the farm buildings and the three of us left, accompanied by a dog, to return to the spot where I'd left my car.

As I started on the journey back to town I felt happy about the Macks and realized that they had given me, unknowingly, a new view of life, of the balance of nature, and of the age-old rights of man and beast.

CHAPTER FIFTEEN

The Heavy Heart

The people on the mountain beyond the little town of Hillside had not been visited for more than three years, which was illegal, an annual visit being considered a necessity by Government standards. The reason for this neglect was the obvious difficulty of reaching the half-dozen houses scattered on the mountain across the river beyond the town. Hillside was a white railway settlement. The mountain beyond had been homesteaded by Indians.

No worker had been found able or willing to cope with the transportation problems. It was necessary to leave early in the morning, following the main highway to a little side road that led eventually to a small settlement about ten miles away. A car could not be used for approximately the last half mile, since the road deteriorated into a bridle path. There were one or two people to be visited at the settlement, then a steep descent to the railway tracks and a 3¹⁄₂-mile walk along the tracks to Hillside. There was one lonely house along the tracks, occupied by an old man who acted as caretaker. He lived there alone, with only an occasional visitor or trip to town on the workmen's small scooter, drowning his lonely sorrows in wine or whiskey. There was always the possibility that he would be in poor condition from one or the other, but – if in moderate shape – he was an interesting old man. At one time educated, his stories of the past were lucid and often extremely funny. Notified in advance of a worker's visit, he always had stewed coffee ready and two pies made from local wild fruits, the choices depending on the season. Pie and coffee consumed and necessary papers signed, the remaining walk along the railway had to be completed.

Everything, even local residents and incoming mail, arrived at Hillside by train. Freight was packed up the mountain by horses: there was no other way of getting anything up. On reaching her destination, if the worker was lucky, Indians on horseback would meet her with a spare horse. The river had then to be forded, the horse carefully picking its way over the rocky river bottom. Then followed a frightening ride along ledges cut in the mountainside. One prayed that the horse was sure-footed. Visiting the half-dozen homes involved a further 10- or 15-mile journey before returning to Hillside village.

Very few workers would tackle this journey. The majority, fresh from the city and college, saw the excursion as difficult, if not impossible. But for me, a country woman at heart, a long horseback ride, the opportunity to explore new and fascinating country, and to meet interesting strangers, was little short of seventh heaven. Most of the homes I had to visit housed people who responded to their isolation – slow speaking, quiet, contemplative, and a little fatalistic. The first home I visited was occupied by one elderly man who was also one of the riders accompanying me up the mountain. He had always lived there, growing up with his family, where his father had homesteaded a considerable acreage. He managed to eke out a slender living over the years by raising hogs and selling apples from a family orchard his father had planted. He had a very small cabin, barely adequate for his scant needs. In the next house, half a mile away, the father and mother lived. At the time of my last visit to them the old man was aged ninety-eight but was still working and riding horseback. His wife, almost as old, had been quite ill and, because of her incapacity, she was entitled to a larger pension than she had been receiving.

Their house was bigger than that of the son I had just visited. There were no luxuries; no carpets other than three braided rugs, well worn by long service. There was a large kitchen stove, and I wondered how that had been carried up the mountain – in sections, no doubt. All furnishings – table, chairs, cupboards, and (seen through an open door) beds – were handmade from wood collected in the area. In spite of the paucity of furnishings, the house had a friendly, homelike feel to it. However, today when we arrived at the house, I was asked if I would mind waiting outside for a short time, because there was some business being contracted within and the lawyer was about to leave. So I tied up my horse and explored the outdoor landscape until voices beyond the house told me that the lawyer was departing, also on horseback. At this time I was not informed of the nature of the business. I was then invited into the home.

The usual coffee was made, but knowing that food would be a problem up there, I had taken my own sandwich lunch. In addition to the old couple present at the interview was another son, referred to by his father as 'the boy', although he was almost seventy years old. 'The boy' had a separate cabin a short distance from the main house. He too raised hogs and, since he was still 'young', had occasional jobs in the village. Business concluded I enjoyed my sandwich and coffee and we talked, slowly and ponderously, with long intervals of complete silence. The nature of the business with the lawyer was disclosed. It appeared that 'the boy' had developed severe heart trouble and could no longer remain at the altitude of the family home. The old couple could not be left alone and he could not stay to help them, so on the advice of friends they were selling the property and moving to a larger town where there was medical help. Apparently the projected move was heartbreaking for the old couple. And, as was so often the case, the property had been sold to a white man for much less than its real value.

It was obvious that the grief of the old man was deep, causing speech to be cumbersome and slow. Suddenly he turned and looked straight at me, eyes clouded with tears, and said that this would be our last visit together. Then he added: 'I have a parting gift for you.' He left the room and returned quickly, holding something in both his hands. Placing the gift on the table, he said: 'This is a rock. It is shaped almost exactly like a heart, and you will notice it is very heavy. So, you see, I give you on parting my heart, which is very heavy at having to leave my land and my home and your visits.'

Then 'the boy' rose, saying: 'I, too, have a parting gift for you.' He left and apparently entered his own little cabin. When he returned, like his father holding his gift in both hands, he presented me with a battered coffee tin which, when opened, showed rather dirty medicated cotton, and resting on this were a number of very nice Indian arrowheads.

'You see,' he said, 'you can take with you a little of our land and some of our tradition.'

All four of us stood silently, staring at the heart-shaped rock and the arrowheads, tears in our eyes.

I had a long way to go and other calls to make, so I was obliged to leave. We shook hands in silence and quietly I found my horse and the companions to help me along the treacherous road to the village. I never saw my friends again since they moved to another area. But, thankfully, I still have the heavy heart for lost land and little bits of that land in the old coffee tin.

CHAPTER SIXTEEN

The Bear

As I drove north from town in an attempt to visit the Maple family I noticed that the waters in the stream on my right hand were higher than usual for the time of year. Then I remembered that a few days ago there had been a number of late thunderstorms, both up in the mountains and in the valleys, which would mean considerable run-off of storm water and heightened river levels. The stream I was following on my right hand went under the road several miles ahead of me and continued its journey to my left. The Maple farm resided on the far side of the stream which meant fording the water. My mind raced ahead of the car, and I wondered if the stream would be passable so soon after the storms. Naturally the only thing to do was wait and find out. Mrs Maple had written to say that a four-year-old granddaughter had come to live with her and she needed help to support this child. Her need, she said, was quite desperate. Hence my early appointment.

As I approached the turn-off road that led to the stream that I must cross, I discovered that my apprehensions were well-founded. The water was quite high over the ford. So I decided to test it in my usual way. Removing shoes and stockings, rolling up clothing round my waist, I stepped into the decidedly chilly water to walk across. From past experience I knew that, if the water was up to a certain height on my legs, the car could not make it without flooding the interior. Today this was the case. So back to the car to collect necessary papers, shoes and stockings, and a small towel, and again into the stream carrying the necessities.

During the first check of the water, I had heard gunfire across the stream and, apparently, near the house that I was to visit. Imagination running in various directions, I wondered what was in store for me on the hill. But all was quiet during my second crossing.

Feet dried, shoes and stockings restored, I picked up my papers and started up the hill on the other side of the stream. About half-way up I noticed in a pool of muck the unmistakable footprint of a large bear. Looking around carefully I failed to see any sign of the monster, so I proceeded on my way with a little more hope than courage.

Approaching the house, I noted a curious odour, not at all pleasant, and unmistakably a scent of blood or raw flesh. Suddenly, on the right, there was the house with three or four very small children running around. And suspended upside down, tied to a branch by his back legs, was a very large bear, dead, with two men working at the removal of his hide.

One of the two men stopped, stared at me, then remarked that it was a good thing I was a little late. Had I been 45 minutes earlier, I might have encountered 'him' (pointing at the half undressed bear) along my road to the house. Then he added: 'By the way, where did you leave your pickup?' I told him that there was no pickup – that I had come in an ordinary passenger car which I'd left on the other side of the stream. 'She's running pretty full', the man said, 'so we didn't expect you. We knew you couldn't drive across – or if you tried, we'd have to pull you out.' I told them my method of testing the water. They seemed to find it very funny.

I turned my attention from the smelly bear's carcass to Mrs Maple and her needs. We entered the house, and I assisted her in filling out necessary forms of application. She explained that she and her husband already had three small children under five years of age, that her daughter had died and the grandchild was to live with her, becoming part of her family in this remote setting. She then told me that there were a few bears around the neighbourhood, but none had ventured so near the house as had this one. Killing him would be allowed because he was a danger to the four small children. I remarked that it was a shame that such a beautiful animal could not have been captured by the rangers or forest service and removed to a place far away where both the bear and the children would be safe. Mrs Maple agreed, said that she hated to see him hanging there, but they hadn't dared to wait until the authorities had time to move him. 'After all,' she said, 'perhaps it is a case of survival of the fittest.'

I glanced through the window at the four little children – one still unable to walk steadily, it was so much a baby – and I wondered whether the two older children were suffering at all from shock at the sight of the dead bear and what were their thoughts, if they had any. I also questioned whether by invading the privacy of these mountains, a privacy long held, the human race was destroying the primitive rights of the animal world. Or, I asked myself, on an already over-crowded planet, was it necessary for wildlife to adjust to every invasion of what was formerly their kingdom?

As I prepared to leave, I noticed that one of the men had brought a pickup round to the front of the house. So I was to be driven back to my car across the river. The man was still laughing. He said: 'You know, I think you are one lucky woman that you didn't come less than an hour ago. Otherwise that bear might have had you hung up by your back legs by now.' Then he added: 'So you waded across the stream. How did you know it wouldn't be too deep for *you*?' I told him that I had forded it before and knew roughly how much water was at this stage of flooding. The man roared with laughter again and added 'Well, you're a one!' as he helped me into my car and prepared to leave, back over the stream.

Again I wondered about fading rights of wildlife as opposed to the needs, safety, and expansion of human life in a diminishing world. As usual my visit had left me with so many questions and so few answers.

CHAPTER SEVENTEEN

The Fisherman

Tom Pritchard lived in a tiny house consisting of one room, a sort of cupboard that he used as a bedroom, and a rather primitive bathroom he had built himself. The house was in a small village near a river and was at the corner of a road climbing up from the river and into the mountains. It was really a beautiful spot with views down the hill to the river and across to very high hills that seemed intent on sliding back down in the valley below.

Mr Pritchard was a fisherman. He spent half his life fishing and the other half making very beautiful small insect-like things as bait, called lures. Tom was quite an artist and had wooden boards to which his bait collection was fastened. He liked to bring out these boards and show them to his few visitors with well-deserved pride. He was a very small man, and while not giving one the impression that he was overly thin, was a slender 5ft 2in with sparkling eyes and quick movements.

Tom's life had been quite unusual. Horses had been his first love, fishing having usurped that love in later years. As a young man, Tom had been a successful jockey. He told me that he had made and spent quite a lot of money. For his mother, he said, he bought a small carriage and a spanking pair of white high-stepping horses. He remembered with a sense of pride that, with his mother at his side, he drove through the local town and out into the country, his spirited horses almost dancing along the way.

The horses, carriage, and mother lasted several years, her place finally being lost to a wife. The marriage did not last very long, but produced one daughter. Tom was short-tempered, mercurial, and had probably been difficult to live with. Later Tom was thrown from a mount. The fall resulted in a badly smashed leg and other injuries, so he was never again able to ride as a jockey.

I was given to understand that his injuries used up most of his money and how he lived after that I was never sure. I think he just drifted. His daughter was raised precariously, occasionally by Tom but mostly by other relatives. As she grew, she became more and more aware of her father's fall from his former grandeur and his apparent inability to rise again. By the time she was in her middle teens or even younger she resented him and rarely contacted him. She was bitter at the fact that he was now an old age pensioner doomed to live his older years in a shabby run-down cottage by a river.

On the occasions of my rare visits to Tom I found him to be a very interesting, lively, and sensitive old man. As time passed it seemed to me that the daughter was missing out on what could be a fascinating friendship with an unusual father. Tom followed the years of development of his daughter quite closely through the rare letters and relatives. She married, and after her child entered school decided to complete her education. She went to college, gained her teaching certificates and accreditation and became a well-liked teacher in a high school. Tom was very proud of her and wished that they would meet. It is possible that he used his passion for fishing as a support of his loneliness.

My business visit to Tom usually took place in the late autumn when the steelhead were running. A number of times he caught a large steelhead immediately before my visit and then handed it to me asking me if I would take it to town and get it smoked. He did not like the fresh fish he caught.

The delivery of the smoked fish was often amusing. I passed the entrance to the road leading to Tom's village in my travels north to other appointments. Occasionally Tom would meet me, waiting sometimes half a day at the junction of a main highway and the side road to the village, and I would deliver the fish. He always carried a large sharp knife and adequate wrappings and insisted on cutting off a small piece of the smoked fish and handing it to me for my trouble and consumption. Then armed with the small piece of fish, I continued on my way. In this doubtful manner I too became a fisherwoman.

As time passed I became more convinced that this strange little man and his daughter should know one another. He always read her few letters to me. Then one day, seeing the envelope near me on the table, I copied her address. This was very strictly none of my business bur I wrote her a short note and told her she had a very lonely father who adored her and was longing to meet her. I added that she was missing out on an important part of her life by refusing to visit him.

After a little while I received a reply from the young woman thanking me very much for my note and telling me that she had decided to take my advice and visit her father. The two, father and daughter, arranged a date for her visit. After this was completed she wrote to me again thanking me very sincerely for my interference in their lives and that she found her father a fascinating character with whom she did not intend ever again to lose touch.

As time passed the two became very close friends and life was enriched for both. I heard that she even learned to fish.

Since those days, at least twenty-five years ago, this woman has written to me an annual letter always expressing her gratitude that through me she had been granted the knowledge of a very interesting man.

Eventually Tom became ill, had to give up his little cottage, and moved to be near his daughter where he could receive care. There he passed away. As for me, I too gained a friendship; that of Tom's daughter. I never think of fish as particularly romantic, but I must confess my gratitude to them for an emotionally satisfying few years of my life, and even though there is no longer a Tom, after all these years I still hear from his daughter.

CHAPTER EIGHTEEN

Linoleum and the Law

Mrs Long was always tired. This was really not surprising for her husband had died leaving her with eight children. Since death from cancer had been anticipated, he had asked one of his friends to keep an eye on his family after his inevitable departure. Helping them over the rough spots of business and making sure that the widow's public grant was more or less adequate for the family, the friend did a very good job of taking care of the grieving widow. He saw to it that she had eight more children without benefit of matrimony, and without adequate compensation to ensure survival of the second family.

By this time the first family was more or less mature and, with the exception of the oldest son, able to take care of its own needs. The oldest son had been born almost completely blind and stayed with the mother through all the turbulence of the second eight children. He was a bright young man, fascinated by cars and their mechanical needs. What he did not know about carburettors it was unnecessary for anyone to know. He had tunnel vision, that is, he could see spots and small things immediately ahead of him in a tiny area. In this way he could concentrate on the details of a carburettor, be well aware of what was wrong, and know how to repair the damage. It took him a little longer than others might have needed to make such repairs, but he was always in demand locally, earning almost enough for self-support.

After the gift of sixteen children Mrs Long was perhaps justified in being tired. The outside of the small cottage where she continued to live after the death of her husband, who had been a mill worker, was untidy and messy in the extreme. I was never invited into the house, so that its state was left to my imagination. Naturally the second eight children grew and became conscious of the strangeness of their domestic life. One day Mrs Long's fourteen-year-old girl stopped me as I was leaving after an interview with her mother and asked if there was any way in which the family could acquire new linoleum for the one living room, which was also a bedroom for some of them. The family had a small income from Social Security brought up to more adequate proportions by a state grant. In accord with the regulations of that time, the extra income could be used for the purchase of household repairs or for other needs. I told my young questioner of this plan, but informed her that I must examine the existing linoleum and judge whether the purchase was needed. The little girl hesitated for a minute then, assured that her mother was somewhere outside the house, she opened the door and let me look in. There I saw shreds of old linoleum remaining in between the cracks in the floorboards, rather dirty since it was impossible to wash the floor in its present condition. There were two or three bedrolls, but no chest of drawers to hold the clothing and possessions of the family or their private treasures; these resting around the room in dilapidated paste-board containers. The whole place was a soiled shambles, an apology for a home. 'You see,' said the child, 'we cannot invite our friends here, which means that we cannot be entertained in their homes. If only we had new linoleum, we could keep the floor clean and the room would be brightened. We could hide the boxes and invite our friends.'

The whole situation was so deplorable that I almost cried for the misery of it. I told the child to measure the room wall-to-wall and then to go out with their mother and choose new linoleum. The grant could be increased to cover not only the cost of medium-priced linoleum, but also the charge the supplier wold make for laying the new cover. There was huge rejoicing in the family, and I was invited to come and see the changes already effected. When the door was opened I was quite shocked to see a bright clean floor covered with brilliant blue roses climbing with their bright green leaves through a red lattice-work. The horrendous pattern chosen by the family and the strange collection of primary colours gave a new and unexpected glamour to the whole room, so that one forgot the blue roses and the rest of the incongruity.

Now I was able to verify a need for furniture; a chest of drawers to hold clothing and possible treasures, and cots to serve the double purpose of seats during the day and beds at night. A table already existed in the wretched room for which there were no chairs, so several chairs were purchased, as was a bench on which to seat at table the youngest members of the family. When I was invited to inspect the new acquisitions, I noticed that already someone had hung two or three pictures of flowers or country scenes on the once grimy walls, which, in their turn, had been washed. It was also apparent that the sanitation had improved, and no longer did the younger members of the family 'go' when they had to wherever they happened to be. I remarked with praise on the improved appearances of the pre-teenage and teenage children. Hair was now brushed and the owners of the hair were comparatively clean.

After the passage of several weeks it was necessary for me to go by the cottage on my way to another home. I noticed two or three strange children playing with members of the Long family. General improvements continued with or without legally purchased additions. After the passage of a few years, the older members of the second family graduated from high school, and since they were very bright children they obtained work away from home and out of the area. After a few months without these senior members, the entire family moved away from the district and into another county. In a strange way I missed them and felt robbed of the job of the steady and mounting improvements. I never forgot them. They remain clearly in my memory, perhaps because of the sharp shock of colour in the hideous linoleum.

I thought this was the end of the episode which had lasted several years, but one day about ten years later the receptionist informed me that two women were in the front office asking to see me, but refusing to give their names. I was told if they continued to refuse I was in no way obliged to interview them, but my curiosity was too strong and I told the receptionist to bring them to my office. As they entered, I saw there was an older and a younger woman. The older one was smartly dressed in not quite the right style for the age, and she was very much made up – but somehow retained a flair of self-importance. The younger woman was dressed in excellent taste, with suitable business-type suit and shoes, and hair perfectly groomed. There was something vaguely familiar about the older woman, but I couldn't place her. She smiled and informed me that I did not recognize her because after ten years she had changed quite a lot. A sudden flash of memory struck me, and quickly I said: 'Aren't you Mrs Long from the old Langley Mills Yard?'

Suddenly she threw her arms around me and hugged me. 'Yes,

of course,' she said. I was enveloped in a cloud of cheap perfume, but somehow it didn't matter, nor did the heavy make-up. She had a job, she said, and in spite of her age she was still a good-looking woman, even after sixteen children. She was a receptionist in a motel town where they were now living.

The neat and natty young woman accompanying her was the fourteen-year-old who had started the upward trend through her wish for impossibly-patterned linoleum to cover a decaying floor. With such strange security under her feet, that little girl was now a legal secretary to a firm of lawyers in a distant town.

CHAPTER NINETEEN

Rainbows

It had been a long hard day involving a brief visit to another county in order to secure access to a farm situated in my area at the end of the farm road. The terrain was rough and made driving a tiring and complex operation. Now, on my return, I stopped to rest for a few minutes on top of the hill that led steeply down to the long valley through which began the last portion of my journey home. From this point the view seemed endless and quite exciting. Evening was developing its long shadows and the sun had disappeared behind the western hills where I had stopped, but across the valley on the eastern hills there was still much brilliant sunlight for the greater area.

This was a day in spring with late storms still visiting. Such a storm was now fuming its way to extinction. At one spot in the east where a veil of rain hid the countryside, a magnificent rainbow developed on the storm-clad mountain. It dipped from the high sky and terminated in the valley below. Playing with my thoughts I said I had to leave and get down to the valley to get my pot of gold.

Suddenly I had a vision – the valley itself where I had

experienced so much trouble, unhappiness, and later success was my pot of gold. I couldn't put it in the bank but there it was, a shining light in that area of my long years of work. I wound my crooked way down the twisted road into the valley, and memories helped me to collect my golden, rainbow-induced pot.

Once down in the valley memories raced, and I realized the debt I owed to this strangely mixed land. Coming into contact with people of other cultures and other philosophies that were not my own, I yet found in a curious way that they did belong to me, because I had learned to belong to other people, other ways of living and other standards. In that valley I had learned much of the wisdom that ruled the lives of other people, foreign to me at first and not understood yet, after lengthy exposure, I realized other ways of life had their own truths and quite often their own magnificence. For example, I was reminded of the courage required when elderly grandparents found it necessary to accept the responsibility for young children abandoned by their own parents, and did so unquestioningly.

Ideals and perhaps faiths have suffered radical changes over the past years. Life and the job have not been easy. There have been miseries. One hill may be approaching darkness, but there have been many later sunsets and many rainbows and innumerable pots of gold, leading to a fullness of life and understanding and acceptance never encountered in a more regulated and easier employment. I owe gratitude to the beautiful country where I have worked and to the often magnificent people I have met in those strangely mixed days of miseries, some triumphs, and always a widening of life offering other doors to open and pass through to new experiences.